LIKE UNDERGROUND WATER

Like Underground Water

The Poetry of Mid-Twentieth Century Japan

Translated by
NAOSHI KORIYAMA *&* EDWARD LUEDERS

COPPER CANYON PRESS

Copyright © 1995 by Naoshi Koriyama and Edward Lueders.

Publication of this book is supported by a grant from the National Endowment for the Arts and a grant from the Lannan Foundation. Additional support to Copper Canyon Press has been provided by the Andrew W. Mellon Foundation, the Lila Wallace–Reader's Digest Fund, and the Washington State Arts Commission. Special thanks to Toyo University for a grant to assist publication of this book. Copper Canyon Press is in residence with Centrum at Fort Worden State Park.

Poem translations first published elsewhere: "Air Raid" by Yoshihara Sachiko, and "A Guerilla's Fantasy" by Kurada Kio, appeared in *Poetry*, March 1984. "Of Bread and Roses," "Low Tide," "Quite Suddenly," and "An Epigraph," by Yoshihara Sachiko; "In My Garden," "The Palm," "The Sole," "A Distant Mirror," and "Chess," by Shinkawa Kazue; and "Me," "Late Summer," and "Calendar Poem" ("A Poetry Calendar"), by Tada Chimako, first appeared in Edward Lueders, "Three Women Poets of Contemporary Japan," *Weber Studies*, Winter 1995. In an earlier, somewhat different form, "Dead Sun," "Me," "A Poetry Calendar," and "Odyssey or 'On Absence,'" by Tada Chimako, appeared in Makoto & Fitzsimmons, *A Play of Mirrors, Eight Major Poets of Modern Japan*, Oakland Univeristy, Michigan (Katydid Press), 1987.

Library of Congress Cataloging-in-Publication Data

Like underground water : poetry of mid-twentieth century Japan /
translated by Naoshi Koriyama and Edward Lueders.
p.   cm.
ISBN 1-55659-102-0 / ISBN 1-55659-103-9 (paper)
Includes index.
1. Japanese poetry – 20th century – Translations into English.
I. Koriyama, Naoshi, 1926– . II. Lueders, Edward G., 1923– .
III. Lueders, Edward.
PL782.E3L.45 1995
895.6'1508 dc20   95-32541

9 8 7 6 5 4 3 2 1

COPPER CANYON PRESS
P.O. BOX 271, PORT TOWNSEND, WASHINGTON 98368

Acknowledgments

WE ARE GRATEFUL for research and travel funds granted by Toyo University in Tokyo and the University of Utah in Salt Lake City that helped make it possible for us to work together in both locations. The libraries of our universities, together with the library of International House in Tokyo, also assisted on key occasions. Special appreciation is due to the Office of the President of Toyo University for aid in support of publication.

We wish to thank the poets in our collection and, where appropriate, their heirs, for their good wishes and gracious permission to present our translations of the poems to English-speaking readers.

Among the many whose interest in our project helped encourage and direct us during our twelve years of trans-Pacific collaboration, two especially deserve individual acknowledgment here. In his diligent and sharp scrutiny of the full manuscript, Hiroaki Sato offered acute suggestions, many of which we needed. And our warmest thanks go to Deborah Keniston, whose contributions to the final stages of revision and production were essential to the completion of this volume.

N. K. and E. L.

Contents

xiii

Introduction

THE GENESIS of this volume reaches back through a chain of connections to World War II. Our personal involvement in that war and its aftermath cast the two of us as compulsory antagonists. However, in the postwar atmosphere of international accommodation, it brought us together, as collaborators on these translations.

Naoshi Koriyama was one of a group of student survivors from the Ryukyu Islands, the main island of which is Okinawa. They were chosen by the U.S. Department of the Army in the early 1950s to study at the University of New Mexico. As a young teaching assistant there, and an Air Force veteran who had served in Asia, I was assigned to oversee the students' orientation and their advanced training in American English. In the process I learned as much from our give-and-take as they did – perhaps more. My correspondence continued with Naoshi Koriyama, who completed his B.A. in English and returned to Japan to become a professor of English language and literature at Toyo University in Tokyo. As poet-professors on opposite sides of the Pacific, our parallel careers and interests kept our correspondence alive.

In the early 1980s, when Naoshi's enthusiasm for the work of modern Japanese poets led him to translate some favorites to share with me, I was pleased and impressed. Next he asked me to comment on more of his translations and to suggest changes to improve his versions for the eye, ear, and sensibility of an American reader. Before long we discovered that the collaboration, which began as a challenge and mutual pleasure, had expanded into an ambitious project that preoccupied us for over a decade.

It also became clear that the devastating effects of the war were central for Japanese poets just as they were for the Japanese populace. The disruptive transitions imposed on imperialist Japan during the despairing postwar period, highlighted both the people's plight and the poets' plaint in the midcentury course of the nation. Yet that course, consistent in its poetry with most facets of twentieth century Japanese culture, found ways to fuse the ancient and traditional with the modern and innovative.

The war was central to our project in another respect. During the rise of military nationalism from the late 1930s until VJ Day in 1945, the development of modern Japanese poetry was stalled by the tightening of government censorship against Western trends and influences. With very few exceptions, the innovative prewar poets who had turned from the rigid traditional forms of the thirty-one-syllable tanka and its popular shortened form, the five-seven-five syllable haiku, to the use of free verse and modern European models, either fell silent or devoted their art to the national fervor in support of the war. For nearly a decade a virtual vacuum halted the creative advance of Japanese poetry. After 1945, however, there was a gradual restoration of those poets who had suffered oppression during the war, their work now characterized by postwar rumination over the war experience and its grim aftermath.

The lapse during the war years was so complete that Ichiro Kono and Rikutaro Fukuda asserted in the introduction to their 1957 *Anthology of Modern Japanese Poetry* that "today, just about a decade after the end of the war, Japanese poetry is hovering just about where it was in 1930." Their estimate now seems a bit severe, for that poetic "hovering" in the 1950s produced a remarkable survey of the psychic landscape below.

Yet their estimate does point up the two most important conditions for the development of Japanese poetry from midcentury on. One is the role of the war and the transition, within some traditional cultural parameters, from the constraints of military totalitarianism to the freedom of the individual in a social democracy. The other is the formidable presence, already established by a generation of venturesome and accomplished prewar poets, of European modernism; in particular, the flexible techniques of free-verse symbolism and surrealism.

The first of these, the transition from wartime to postwar Japan, changed the Japanese métier from militaristic nationalism to economic commercialism. In their poetry, the traditional tanka form, already challenged by the freedom of *vers libre*, was further discredited by its close association with the old imperial regimes, especially with their military elite, including the World War II generals who, when sentenced to execution as war criminals, followed established ritual by writing death poems in the tanka form. Japanese leaders had adapted Western colonial imperialism for their prewar role as self-designated leaders of the Greater East Asia Co-Prosperity Sphere. Japanese poets adapted Western free forms for their aesthetic and cultural role in postwar society.

Some, following the examples of Baudelaire, Rimbaud, and Mallarmé, wrote prose poems. This freed their work not only from fixed metrical form but also from linear versification and intent. The results are among the most abstruse and difficult in modern Japanese poetry.* Some adopted the modes and attitudes of American "beat" poets to project their countercultural sentiments. A number were attracted to the rhythms and improvisatory freedom of American jazz.

Nearly all experimented in one way or another with untried resources of the Japanese language itself. They revolted against the rigid formal language devices of traditional poetry in which the structure was technically strict, intricate, and

---

* For full discussion and examples see Donald Keene, *The Modern Japanese Prose Poem* (Princeton University Press, 1980). The present collection includes prose poems by Irizawa Yasuo, Kokai Eiji, Nakae Toshio, and Kasuya Eiichi.

many-layered. They felt free to take advantage of the natural ambiguities in Japanese, a language rich in suggestion and generally without the restrictive Western distinctions of plurals, specific tenses, and relative pronouns. Their written language is also characterized by strong visual modes of association and suggestion, including the use of *kanji* ideograms (Chinese characters). This emphasis on the power of the visual image also made the special effects of symbolism and surreal imagery particularly inviting to modern Japanese poets.

All these shifts in the language factors, purposes, and techniques at midcentury reflect the postwar emergence of the poet's personal voice and presence in the poem. This stood in clear and conspicuous distinction from the impersonal, reticent indirection of traditional tanka and haiku. Their use of colloquial language also injected the immediacy of individual utterance into the poem. Japanese poetry had no tradition of such direct, unceremonious language. Each poet was free to fashion his or her own voice, form, and demeanor, using whatever suitable models were available, or boldly starting anew. Both the audaciousness and the danger involved are clearly enunciated in this collection by Yamamoto Taro's artistic manifesto, "My Poetry Is Direct." But they are demonstrated to some degree in nearly every poem here. In translation, the conventions of English grammar, syntax, and rhetorical precision can only begin to suggest the palimpsest of associations and dissociations latent in the Japanese language and available to each of these poets for their artful appropriation.

The new individualism befit their counterculturalism, their common themes of isolation, and their revolt against sentimental aestheticism. In at least one respect, however, the emergence of the poet's individual personality was modified by the Japanese penchant for culturally defined patterns of group identity. Traditionally, the Japanese have discouraged the show of individuality. Conformity and cooperation are taught from infancy, and allegiance to one's group is expected. Postwar poets proved no exception. The proliferation of poetry groups after the war helped to channel the mainstream of postwar poetry and to give definition to its tributaries. Each group had its magazine, each magazine its coterie of contributors.

Of prime importance was the Arechi (Waste Land) group stemming from the influential poetry magazine of that name founded before the war by young poets at Waseda University, among them Ayukawa Nobuo. Arechi was revived for a second series (1947–48), and beyond, by poets whose war experience furthered the group's identification with the themes of despair and futility in T. S. Eliot's 1922 poem, from which it took its name. The Retto (Archipelago) group began as a congregation of left-wing *avant-garde* poets concerned with social and political problems in postwar Japan. Other groups with magazines of various types enlisted new and progressively younger postwar generation poets. One of the most influential groups grew up around the eclectic poetry magazine *Rekitei* (Historical

Passage), founded by Kusano Shinpei, who remained a central figure in the group up to his death in 1988.

Along with the increasing number of groups and magazines through the mid-century years, the number of poetry prizes grew. Among the early winners of the prestigious H-Shi (Mr. H) Prize, initiated in 1951, were Tomioka Taeko, Kora Rumiko, and Ishigaki Rin, indicative of the increased presence after the war of women in the ranks of leading poets. Women's poetry magazines, such as *Nobi* (Field Fire), edited by Takada Toshiko, and *La Mer*, edited by Murou Saisi Prize-winners Shinkawa Kazue and Yoshihara Sachiko, did much to give encouragement and recognition to women writing contemporary poetry. The work of women poets contributed markedly to the variety, vigor, and international notice of midcentury poetry in Japan.

The overall patterns of these literary historical developments outlined for us the shape and the limits of this volume. We begin in the 1930s at the peak of pre-war surrealist poetry, before the imperial government censorship proscribed Western tendencies.

We open with the poems of Nishiwaki Junzaburo, whose collection *Ambarvalia* (1933), preceded by the quarterly *Shi to Shiron* (Poetry and Poetics, 1929–1931) and followed by the advent of the long-lived magazine *Rekitei* in 1935, consolidated the early influence of European modernism. At the end of our collection are poets born no later then the 1930s. Thus we limit our selection to poets with at least childhood recollections of the World War II era, those harrowing years when human hope in Japan, as in its poetry, was held in suspension – to borrow the presiding image from Ooka Makoto's ardent poem that gives us our title – like underground water.

Edward Lueders
Salt Lake City, Utah

LIKE UNDERGROUND WATER

Nishiwaki Junzaburo | (1894–1982)

NISHIWAKI JUNZABURO, one of Japan's outstanding contemporary poets and an influential literary critic, was born in Ojiya, Niigata Prefecture. He had a talent for drawing and wanted to be an artist, but his father's death led him to study economics at Keio University. He did, however, study the literature of foreign countries, notably the work of Ezra Pound, T.S. Eliot, and the French symbolists. When he was abroad in England in 1922, he encountered the modern literary movements of surrealism, cubism, and imagism. He met T.S. Eliot, and in 1925 published *Spectrum*, a collection of poems in English. *Fukuikutaru Kafu yo!* (*You, Fragrant Fireman!*), an anthology he compiled in 1927 with six other poets, was the first book of surreal poetry published in Japan. Besides writing in Japanese, Nishiwaki wrote a considerable amount of poetry in English and French.

New Year's Day

Ah,
man has again completed
his circling of the sun,
turning round and round
together with forests and foxes,
bush warblers and five-storied pagodas,
coal and agate,
carp and saury-pike, too,
fire and water and air and earth.
Everyone who has been far away
comes back to his native mulberry farms.
The tinker and the woodcutter too, coughing,
hurry home, out of breath.
Humans worship gods of mountains and rivers,
sprinkling *sake* on the ground.
The chieftain and the principal too
are guzzling *sake* from a bowl.
I'll go and make a New Year's call on a friend.
In front of the cigarette shop on Koshu highway,
a drunken old mother is chewing on an orange.
A yellow dog peers this way.
When I go down the slope, bushes close in
like angry waves.

A fog of five colors hangs in the air.
Ah, this new field again goes sinking
toward the sun,
in order to create a new oval myth!

The Sun

The countryside of Calmojin produces marble.
There I once spent a summer.
There are no skylarks, no snakes around.
Only the sun rises out of the bush of green plums
and sinks again into the bush.
A boy caught a dolphin in the brook and laughed.

Shepherd of Capri

Even in the spring morning
my Sicilian pipe makes a sound of autumn,
tracing thoughts for several millenniums back.

Kaneko Mitsuharu | (1895–1975)

KANEKO MITSUHARU was born in Aichi Prefecture. He began to write poetry at age twenty-two. After a year in England and Belgium (1919–1921) he returned to Japan and published *Koganemushi* (*A Golden Beetle*, 1923). Later travel in China, Southeast Asia, and Europe added to his growing sense of alienation and his opposition to imperialism. During World War II Kaneko was the only major Japanese poet to write and publish antiwar poems. His postwar collections, notably *Rakkasan* (*Parachute*, 1948), *Ningen no Higeki* (*The Tragedy of Man*, 1952), and *Suisei* (*The Force of Water*, 1956), experimented with poems of earthy lamentation and veiled erudition.

Reed

Out of the water, reaching for the sky,
a reed stands.
The reed quivers.
From its straight stalk,

to the end of the blade
it quivers delicately,
like a quivering javelin
stuck in the ground.

Between the fresh water
and the seawater,
the swaying reed,
now bending over, now rising,

rubs the boat's side,
and the movement of the boat
expands the water's rings,
making the sleeping reeds rustle,

flooded halfway
in the water,
a thousand, tens of thousands of them,
one after another.

Ah, the water of autumn has never touched
my heart and eyes
so deeply
as this year.

Pushing aside the roots of the reeds
submerged at the bottom,
my boat and I proceed,
as if invited

by the smell of water
under the flying clouds,
torn apart and broken,
spread out over the water.

Releasing me from
the fifty and some years
which held me,
the boat carries me around,

And drifts about
letting me amuse myself.
Lying in the bottom of the boat
now I meditate.

The fifty and some years
that have flowed away from me
spread out over
and beyond the sandbank of reeds,

and look indistinguishable.
Anyway
what had happened?
What things had occurred?

Pushed around by the flow of time
like the flow of water,
I was carried away by the unexpected swiftness
of the current through the depths.

At the mercy
of the tangle of love and hatred,
I had no time to see things,
now floating, now sinking.

But that's not surprising.
Nothing but the gentleness
of women
has had any significance to me.

Everything else is an empty act
just like wind
blowing from one reed blade
to another.

A woman with her thin arms bent
like two flower stalks
in a glass,
chuckling at me,

a woman casually met,
who deftly avoided me,
without even looking back, drifting away.
Women were flowers, all of them.

The water
carried them along.
where to?
God only knows.

When fifty and some years
have flowed away,
how light I feel,
I who have shed everything.

How infused with light I am!
Just ask the heart traveling
over the water,
"Is there still any rebelliousness left?"

Song of a Sad Pearl Diver

Fighting against my own body's buoyancy,
I dive
toward the bottom of the glaring water.

I go looking for a beautiful shellfish and a
bead said to have been made of a tear.

The sea all around me turns
like a glass ball.
Confusing the upside with the downside, I struggle
to put the bubbling South Pacific
back to its original position.

Along the aberrated boundaries
of currents cold and warm,
I reach down, in distorted posture,
risking my life.

There, a spring is spouting faintly
in the shade of a rock at the bottom,
and beautiful seashells seclude themselves
to put on makeup;

there a weaving scorpion fish
and a baby striped beak perch
come out to play,
trailing their own shadows behind;

there a man-eating shark is hanging around,
watching,
casting a sharp, sidelong glance from a distance
like a spy of the secret police.

Tearing the water like a razor,
spouting bubbling water
at my fingertips,
I look for a weeping seashell.

The most beautiful bead,
which can brighten the night itself –
I can hand it over
to the merchant working his abacus,
with a cigarette in his mouth,

to the merchant
who can make an enormous profit
just by valuing his goods
and handing them over to the purchasers.

The cold-hearted women
who tease their men
for these grains of truth
taken at the risk of my neck,

wear them stringed
on their stone-like
pulseless breasts,
just for their vain pride.

Murano Shiro | (1901–1975)

MURANO SHIRO was born in the suburbs of Tokyo. He studied economics and German at Keio University and after graduation began a successful lifelong career in business. He was first attracted to poetry by reading the German impressionist poets, and he joined several poetry magazine groups, including the modernist Bungaku group. He translated works by German writers and, with other poets, edited the magazines *Shiho* (*Poetic Technique*, 1933–34), *Shinryodo* (*New Territory*, 1937–42), and *Gendai Shi* (*Modern Poetry*, 1948–). His own books of poetry, *Taiso Shishu* (*Poems about Gymnastics*) and *Boyo Ki* (*Records of Lost Sheep*), won prizes. In *Taiso Shishu* he created dynamic physical movements of sporting human bodies with vivid athletic imagery. Much of his other poetry depicts life beset by existential anxieties. Murano twice served as president of the Modern Poets' Association of Japan.

Pole Vault

He comes running like a wasp,
carrying a long pole,
and quite naturally floats into the sky,
chasing the ascending horizon.
When he finally goes over the limit,
he throws away what has supported him.
There's nothing for him but to fall.
Oh, helplessly he falls.
Now, on top of the runner who has just tumbled to the ground
in such a miserable way,
the horizon suddenly descends
and hits him hard on the shoulders.

About Sketching

What I'm trying to draw is:
a tree –
a mold of twisted experience
that is burned, faltering
on the hill
of scorching debris –

illusions of wretched Minerva
swarming like butterflies
over the branches and tops of trees
which will never blossom.
I open my snow-white palette
in the shade of a tall nettle,
and shed unexplainable feelings
together with hot tallow,
not out of pity,
not out of love,
only for the truth,
only for my limited canvas.

Horizontal Bar (1)

By the seashore
I see poor octopuses hung on wooden racks.
I too am hung in the air.
A temporary iron bar supports me.
A thought descends
and runs out of my nose.
I hiccup,
kick up the landscape,
and dare to blaspheme the sky.
Then it puts me
on a new world.
I look down for the first time
upon the surprised faces,
upon the treetops comically shortened.

Horizontal Bar (11)

I jump at the horizon.
My fingertips barely catch it.
I hang on the world.
My muscles are all I can count on.
My color reddens. My body contracts.
My legs go up.

Oh, where am I going?
The world makes a huge turn,
and I am up above.
I look down from high up.
Ah, a soft cloud touches my shoulders.

Saga Nobuyuki | (1902–)

SAGA NOBUYUKI was born in Miyazaki Prefecture. From 1923 to 1945, he worked for a publishing company. He did not begin to write poetry in earnest until after World War II, when he joined the Rekitei group. Later he became the longstanding editor of *Shigaku* (*Poetics*). Among his books are *Ai to Shi no Kazoeuta* (*Counting-out Rhymes of Love and Death*, 1957) and *Tamashii no Naka no Shi* (*Death in the Soul*, 1966). Saga's themes are the familiar ones of life, death, love, time, and eternity; his approach is inventive, his style austere.

Fire

Please don't put it out, ever –
the fire that moves out of me into you.
It is the only fire in my life.
A large bird has swooped down into the deep valley
between death and me and plucked it up.
That little fire demands nothing of you.
It protects you with perfect selflessness,
obstructing anyone's approach toward you.
And now you stand stark naked
holding up the fire on the stairway –
on the endless stairway leading to the room upstairs.

The River of Life

We sometimes want to make sure
of what we have learned, somehow, once again.
We trace the outline of an obscure thing
lying too far away, in a serene, sincere color.
Then the dense fog suddenly clears.

Now in front of us a large gate suddenly looms up.
By the shore of the river of life flowing swiftly by,
the surface glitter of the river lights up the tall gate
and our hands.

The lines we have been tracing begin
to sound unexpectedly like the strings of a harp,
and we feel that the second, faraway world is
now already around us.

In the strings of the harp reaching toward the end of the sky
we feel infinite coolness.
As everything greatly sways in complete harmony,
we, too, move responsively in small waves.
Now the figure of the being holding the strings at great distance
appears and disappears in the fog drifting by.

A Woman Before Eve

When I got there,
the Earth had already begun to turn.
When I fell asleep, it was tracing time backward from that point.
There was a dead woman on it.
On the Earth gliding aslant in its new orbit,
I met the very first death of a human.
I could not endure the immeasurable loneliness in the face
of the dead woman, who had not known anything, even laughing or crying.
Soon I too began to turn quietly.
And the Earth with the woman on it got farther and farther away from me.

Kusano Shinpei | (1903–1988)

KUSANO SHINPEI was born in Fukushima Prefecture. He went to Kuangchou, China, in 1921 and studied at Leinang University. He started a poetry magazine, *Dora* (*The Gong*) there in April 1925, but returned to Japan in July due to anti-British and anti-Japanese movements. He went to China again in 1943 and returned to Japan in 1946. Kusano started the poetry magazine *Rekitei* in 1935 and remained a central figure in that group until his death. In 1928 he published *Daihyaku Kaikyu* (*The One Hundredth Class*), a book of poems presenting his anarchistic view of human life through the eyes of a frog. *Kaeru* (*Frogs*), was published in 1938. Kusano wrote many poems about Mt. Fuji as well. Besides poetry, his works include translations, anthologies, essays, and an autobiography. *Mt. Fuji*, his selected poems in English translation, was published in 1991 by Katydid Books, Oakland University, Michigan.

The Moon

As I dip my body in the bathtub late at night
a charming moon, as plump as a maiden,
streams in through the window
and carelessly touches my body,
entwining herself around me seductively, tenderly.

Mt. Fuji Poem No. III

Ever since the beginning
through billions of days and black nights
sits the stupendous body in the hollowness of immense time.

Ah, as for me,
I have humbly sung small songs
in my countless encounters with it.
And far beyond my praise,

far in the distance,

sits the impressive
Fuji's body –
a stern, white, great spirit.

Mt. Fuji Poem No. XVII

100 million years from now,
at the end of tens of billions of years,
life on Earth may all die out –
trees, grasses, birds, frogs, and humans too,
even all the lichens, sea slugs too.
Only notches and creases of blue ice will remain.
Everything will change completely.
But Mt. Fuji will sit stern for a while after all the change.
What formidable beauty that didn't even exist in the Age of Fire!
The ghosts of the Japanese
will gather and freeze there.
It will spout a white flame
from its crest.
Heaven will come down silently to witness the rites.

Ono Tozaburo | (1903–)

BORN IN OSAKA, Ono Tozaburo went to Tokyo in 1920 to enter Toyo University, but dropped out in eight months. He stayed for about five years in his boarding house near the university, and became interested in poetry and books about anarchism by Osugi Sakae and others. His first book of poetry, *Hanbun Hiraita Mado* (*The Half-Opened Window*, 1926), showed his repulsion from bourgeois complacency and his aversion to state authority, government power and militarism. Much influenced by Carl Sandburg's *Chicago Poems*, he published *Proletarian Poems of America*, 1931, a book of translations in collaboration with Kusano Shinpei and Hagiwara Kyojiro. A year earlier he started an anarchistic poetry magazine, *Dando* (*The Line of Fire*), with Akiyama Kiyoshi. After World War II he was published in many magazines and conducted a creative writing program called the "Osaka School of Literature."

Eel

The thick piles of the wharf
are driven into the sea,
as deep as telephone poles upside down.
Heavy waves heaving in over the evening sea
keep washing the bridge pier on which oil, mud, and barnacles
    stick black.
On the opposite shore, flares stand thick.
Their tall, slender chimneys
send up crimson flames
into the purple-hued sky.
There is an angler on the windy jetty.
The angler turns his lonely back to me,
hanging his legs over the jetty.
To be by the side of an angler
is to wait patiently with him
for a long, long time, like an eternity,
looking at a point on the surface of the sea;
yet it can be the rarest opportunity.
As I come close to his back,
an eel, like a huge sea serpent, is lifted, tracing a trajectory.
This thing that has dwelled in the pit
at the bottom of the dark sea

at the foot of the pier covered thick with oil, mud, and barnacles
being pounded by the evening waves,
now reveals its white belly once or twice,
dancing in the air,
and then comes thrown at my feet
together with the fishing rod.

Someone Waiting

There
is someone waiting.
In a chair of the waiting room with night winds blowing through,
at an unmanned station in the field,
he is left alone,
dressed like a traveler,
waiting for me.
On the highway I'm walking along
the noontime sun is still shining,
the sky is bright,
and thistles are blooming on the sides of the road.
While it's not known when I will arrive at the station,
he is waiting indefinitely,
waiting with his eyes fixed on the floor.
On his lap lies a heavy bag.
In the bag
are a cake of soap, a towel, a spare shirt,
and a safety razor with the blade in place, well-used by me.
In other words, he is waiting
with everything ready for my daily life,
just as it should be.
At the foot of the mountain on the other side of the valley,
I see the hole of an abandoned silver mine.
The entrance is half-covered with grass.
Going down the valley,
I walk toward that place.
Though I linger as long as I can,
wasting my time on the road,

I am steadily approaching that person
who is waiting for me.
Ah, Death.

A White Horse

Riding on the wind,
the spray of waves falls
over the road in the mountains and rivers of Chungcheng Dong, Korea.
A white horse walks, hanging its head low,
by the evening seashore,
where not a soul is seen.
Across its bare back, the horse carries
a prostrate man in a prison uniform.
His dangling hands are tied,
almost reaching the ground.
The blood dripping along his fingers
falls, dotting the sand.
I know not where the horse is going.
It just keeps walking down the long, long, deserted beach,
carrying the man on its back,
bathed in the spray.
The man on the horse hangs upside down
with his head down,
but opening his eyes wide,
he looks at the waves of the Sea of Japan,
beating against the Korean evening with thumps
from under the horse's belly.
Even when night comes,
the figure of the horse walking by the shore is white.
It never disappears.

Yamanoguchi Baku | (1903–1963)

YAMANOGUCHI BAKU was born in Naha, Okinawa. He went to Tokyo, hoping to become a poet or an artist in 1922, but because of the devastating earthquake the following year, he went back to Okinawa. He returned to Tokyo in 1926. Determined to write poetry, he worked at many odd jobs while he kept writing. Many of his poems are set in his native Okinawa. His style is simple, conveying his daily experiences, thoughts, and feelings with disarming frankness and humor.

A Scene on Okinawa

In the yard over there
fighting cocks are always hungry for blood.
Each one struts
in his cage,
perking up his shoulders,
looking quite self-confident,
waiting impatiently
for the day he'll fight.
The old man of the Akamine family sits
at the edge of the veranda each morning,
holding his tobacco tray,
and looks over to see if his cocks are well.
This morning, as usual, he's at the edge of the veranda.
His pipe must have plugged up
and he bangs it on the tray.
The fighting cocks raise their heads
in unison
at the sound.

A Game Nobody Won

In the jostle of the crowded train
I had my wallet picked.
I was mad at the loss of the wallet,
but I felt like laughing
at myself for being so mad.
I felt like soothing my foolishness,

saying, "Well, cool down, man."
The fact was, I didn't have much money
to keep in the wallet,
but my wallet was almost bursting
with all the name-cards of people.
By now the pickpocket in turn may be mad
at the wallet full of name-cards
instead of money,
looking foolish himself.
The guy may have stealthily tossed the wallet
out of the train window
over the railroad bridge.

A Funeral

While I was trudging around,
just borrowing money all the time,
I died
one day.
People were saying,
"So that guy's dead at last, huh?"
They came to my funeral
to bid me farewell
with their palms folded, and left, one after another.
Thus I've come to the other world
only to find my son, looking disgruntled,
waiting for me.
I ask him what he's so grouchy about.
He says he hasn't been offered any good food
at the *Bon* Festival.
To soothe him I pat him
on the head.
When it dawns on me
that even dead people want things that cost money,
it's just like being alive back on Earth,
and the other world
    and the world on Earth seem no different.

NOTE: The Bon Festival occurs in mid-August, when the Japanese offer
    food and drink to the souls of their ancestors.

Makabe Jin | (1907–1984)

MAKABE JIN was born in Yamagata City in the northern part of Japan, At fifteen he began to write poetry and while still quite young read Whitman's *Leaves of Grass*. A farmer by trade, Makabe knew the joys and sorrows of the farmer's life in the harsh realities of rural northern Japan. He formed a farmers' union and fought for farmers' rights. His books include *Machi no Hyakusho* (*The Peasant in the City*, 1932), *Aojishi no Uta* (*Song of a Blue Wild Boar*, 1947), and *Nihon no Fudo nitsuite* (*On the Climate of Japan*, 1958). He wrote about farmers' lives, and the mountains, rivers, and villages in a powerful and straightforward style.

On the Damp Climate of Japan

The island running from north to south was
once the eastern edge of Eurasia.
It was connected with the Himalayan Kunlun.
The inland plant community once extended all the way to here.
Straits couldn't have been boundaries for birds and beasts.
Winds must have blown here from deserts.
Our physiology, however, does not remember the light and winds
of remote ancient times.
We cannot remember the scraping of glaciers
or the tremors of the sunken lands.
We don't even know the day when this island became an island.
The Sea of Japan –
it is a spindle-shaped salt lake suddenly formed by sinking land.
Even the few remaining land bridges crumbled,
and we dream of the moment when the Liman Current with its icebergs
and the Equatorial Current leaped into the hollow
from the straits at the north and south.
Forests still green clung
to the submerged sunken mountains,
wavering like water weeds....

What our physiology does remember is fog and rain.
The landscape has always been damp.
The island frequently spewed up fire, turning the land surface red with lava,
but that has never been able to dry up the assaulting fog.
Ever-resounding circular currents, cold and warm, kept washing the shores,

and oceanic air masses always came round, blown by seasonal winds, making
   green lichens thrive.
The land retains countless sea lakes and sunken crater lakes.
Water lies latent everywhere.
Water keeps flowing from the mountains into the sea.
Lowlands sometimes turn into boundless marshlands.
We can remember the feel of earthenware from the *Jomon* period,
the heat and light of fire struck with flint.
While the polished stone played the crudest role,
our physiology developed like vegetables –
just like vegetables.
How much change have we undergone since then?
Anyway, we have lived in houses made of wood and grass.
Looking at the light through paper windows,
some of us still cherish the fundamental form
of each day's feeling.

The fog is dense,
swallowing up the view.
Fog even oozes out of our skin.
We even looked for mineral veins in the fog,
dug coal mines and oil wells,
generated electricity.
But the landscape we have, when the fog clears,
is a field of weeds all over,
no pieces of iron visible anywhere.
We mistreat ourselves in the fog.
We turn in upon ourselves in the fog.
Still, the Earth might undergo violent changes at any moment.
This time the undersea mountains, long oblivious to the sun's heat,
may begin to rise and rise,
and the folded Tien Shan Mountains might collapse,
shaken by the wave-like motions of the Earth's crust,
filling up the Sea of Japan.

NOTE: The *Jomon* is an archaeological period in Japan, lasting between
   approximately 10,000 B.C. and 4 B.C., during which earthenware had
   straw-rope patterns on it.

A Mountain Pass

A mountain pass demands a decision of us.
The bright melancholy of parting hangs on the mountain pass.
One who has climbed to the top of the pass
exposes himself to the overhanging blue,
soon turning his back to it.
Two landscapes are stitched together there,
but we cannot enter into one
without losing the other.
Only by sustaining a great loss
can we have a new world open.
When we stand at a mountain pass,
the path we came by looks dear
and the way ahead lovely.
The way makes no response.
The way ahead only looks infinitely enticing.
The sky above looks sweet as aspiration.
One has to part with one world
there
when he has decided on his destination.
To bury the thought
the traveler now leisurely urinates,
now plucks some grass,
now takes a puff on a cigarette,
absorbing as much of the landscape as he can.

Estuary

The river quickly loses enthusiasm
where it empties itself into the sea.
It forgets its adventures at cliffs, its passion in the canyons.
The river that has hurried noisily along its way,
swirling,
gliding,
now ends its journey in confusion here.
The sea swells.
Waves jostle and leap.
The river slows down.

Thwarted by the piles of debris it has brought down,
it timidly skirts the delta.
It crawls out to the beach and gets sucked up by the sand.
Only the grasses, strong in the sand, open their heads on the shore.
Black birds come in flocks.
Humans languish
when they fall into the hollow of this landscape,
and they build a bridge, bearing the shame,
to extend the road along the shoreline
in a straight line.
Night comes.
In the wind sweeping up the river valley a little way
the water awakens,
regaining its resistant force.

Dobashi Jiju | (1909–1993)

DOBASHI JIJU was born in Yamanashi Prefecture. He spent nine years (1924–1933) in America. As he worked his way through Hamilton High School in San Francisco and took college courses at night, he read the poetry of Murou Saisei (1889–1962) and Carl Sandburg, and began to write poems himself. He returned to Japan and while working for a newspaper company, he continued to write poetry, and published his first collection, *Flowers*, 1953, at the age of forty-four. His poetry is down-to-earth, forthright, and easy to read. His sixth book of poetry, *Japantown, San Francisco*, 1978, is a collection of exotic and engaging poems about his youthful days in San Francisco.

My Bicycle Bell

Ringing the bell of my bicycle,
I ride through the crowds.
Since I ring the bell persistently,
I never bump into anyone.
Since I don't bump into anyone,
I sometimes want to bump gently into a child
and surprise him.

I want to bump elastically
into a young woman's fresh body.
I want to ride forth over the body of a man
who would not feel pain even if he fell.

But keeping the bell ringing
I pass by without incident.
What a peaceful custom!
What an easygoing sound the bell makes!

But soon
I am stopped
by a train of the Yokosuka Line.
Then I get off my bicycle for the first time
and ring the bell vigorously.
With that,

the train shakes its head
and passes by at full speed.

What an effective bell it is!
(I am surprised
by the pleasant sound it makes.
Amid the rumble and roar
my bell rings with resonance.)

I pass again
through the crowds.

I keep ringing the bell incessantly, until
blood oozes from my fingers,
but I won't let go
of my bell.
No matter how wonderful any other bell may be,
I will keep on ringing mine.

Wrong Words

"Please sleep in peace,
for we will never repeat the mistake."

Who in the world said these words?
For three years since the monument was erected,
I've been looking for the person who said these words,
but in vain.
The bones of housewives, young women and old women, come
out of the graves in and outside the city.
Carrying the bones of young boys along,
they go out every day, taking their lunch with them.
Since they have no sense of distance,
they began by going to America,
then to every corner of Europe,
walking till their white leg bones got stiff.
But they could never find anyone
who said such words –
such earnest,

such unbelievably gentle words.
The bones of the women
got really exhausted at last.
They no longer had any place to search.
(Hiroshima itself is the only place left unsearched,
but the people of Hiroshima
couldn't have said such absurd words.)
Leaning on the boards of their coffins,
the bones heaved a deep sigh,
just like living people.

"Please sleep in peace,
for we will never repeat the mistake."

Perhaps someone said these words
by mistake.
And the mason too, hearing these words,
may have inscribed them on the monument by mistake.

The Endearing Sea

As I lived far away from the sea,
it gradually passed more out of my mind every day,
like its distance.
After days and days,
it became like a dot, no longer looking like a sea.
I felt compelled to go to the movies
to see the sea
on the screen.

But when I slept at night,
the sea came to me, pushing down my chest
and raising clear blue waves.
I just slept, even in the daytime,
freely.
Then
the sea kept mounting big waves
on my chest,
covering me with spray from a storm.

And sometimes it washed up beautiful white bones,
which had sunk to its bottom,
up around my ribs.

Amano Tadashi | (1909–1993)

AMANO TADASHI was born in Kyoto. He began to read European writers in the late 1920s and, after graduation from the First Municipal Commercial High School of Kyoto, submitted stories and poems to the alumni association's literary magazine. While employed from 1928 to 1943 by the Daimaru Department Store of Kyoto he wrote poetry and movie reviews. His first book of poems was *Ishi to Hyo no Katawaranite* (*By the Side of a Stone and a Leopard*, 1932). Many other collections of poems, drawings, and essays followed. With *The Poetry of Amano Tadashi* he won the Mugen Prize in 1975. Amano's poetry typically offers sharp observations beneath a divertingly casual lyrical surface.

At Midnight

"It's troublesome
waking up so often at midnight,"
an aged person grumbles.
"It's a convenient thing, really,"
the other aged person says.
"You know,
it's a most convenient way
to make sure
that you aren't dead, isn't it?"
Then they both
laugh
in hoarse, low voices.

A Hyphen

When you look into a biographical dictionary
you see entries such as *So-and-so* (1903–1950),
meaning the person was born in 1903
and died in 1950.
The hyphen signifies the person's lifetime.
The entry *So-and-so* (1909–   ),
with nothing following the hyphen,
means that the person is still alive.
Whether one is listed in biographical dictionaries or not,

everyone alive has a line dangling from behind his back.
Though it is invisible,
it somehow makes us curious –
the blank after that hyphen.

A Myth

A huge rock slid down a mountain.
A sharp point of light, raising a shriek,
stamped an arabesque pattern
on the top of the rock.
At that very moment, somewhere,
a swallowtail took a deep breath,
silently putting its wings together.
At a maternity hospital in town, at that same time,
destitute Mary gave birth to twins,
and the twins' father cried at the bedside.

At that instant, in a rainy cemetery,
a stray dog sniffed at a flower,
then languidly
trotted away.

Sugawara Katsumi | (1911–1988)

SUGAWARA KATSUMI was born in Miyagi Prefecture, where he studied graphic design at an art school. His first book of verse, *Te* (*Hands*), was published in 1951. After World War II he joined the poetry groups Cosmos, Retto, and Gendishi no Kai. Sugawara was at one time a member of the Japan Communist Party. His poems show a warm, gentle sympathy for human adversity, representative of Japan's left-wing lyric poetry.

Supper

As I am having salted salmon and tea
for supper all by myself,
a yellow moon floats up
above the roof on the other side of the alley.
A snatch of the song "A Tree in the Pot" is heard, as usual, from
    next door,
and the smell of daphnes drifts in from somewhere.
As I eat my meager supper,
such rich friends as these come visiting casually.
Since I am without electric lights from tonight on,
I light a paper lantern, reaching up,
and my shadow expands, filling the whole room.

On the Other Side of the Night

As I listen to the insects,
there seems to be a peaceful world
on the other side of the night,
and they seem to be living
a harmonious life there.
I, too, hope to go through the dark night
to a brighter place.

A Dark Evening

In a room where no other person is around,
my suit hangs all alone.
My own self,
all worn out, hangs on the wall.
Even the electric light looks dim tonight.

The Last Runner

The last one in the race is still running.
It is all he can do just to keep going,
and just a little word spoken to him now
would make him break into tears.
Since there is nothing else to do but run,
should anything enter his mind
he would regret terribly
realizing that what he is doing now
has been a complete mistake.
No other runner is around.
Don't speak to him.
Don't say anything to him.
That person running at the edge of distant time
is no longer even him....

Under the sky, which has suddenly calmed down,
all by himself,
working his chest like a bellows,
there goes the runner from Ceylon now,
the loneliest runner in the world.

Aida Tsunao | (1914–1990)

AIDA TSUNAO was born in Honjo, Tokyo, and studied social science at Nihon University. At fifteen he was deeply impressed by the French surrealist Comte de Lautréamont's nightmarish epic, *Chants de Maldoror*. He also developed an interest in anarchism and Marxism. In 1940 he went to China to work for the Special Service Agency of Nangching. There he met Kusano Shinpei, who suggested he send his poetry to *China–Japan Culture* and other publications. He also worked in Shanghai before his return to Japan in 1946. He joined the Rekitei group in 1947. Aida's first book of verse, *Kanko* (*Saltwater Lake*, 1957), won the Takamura Kotaro Prize. Much of his poetry takes the form of a fable or symbolic narrative, often told with a mildly sardonic tone.

Homecoming

I have returned home at last.
I have come back
to my ruined hometown.
Wheat has grown tall
around the place where my home was burned down.
The wheat has eaten
the ashes.
After relieving myself for the last time
I collapse
like a cicada's shell.
A dog will carry away
my tattered shoes.
My body will decompose
into bits and pieces.
The wheat will now
eat me up.
Grind the wheat, when ripe,
into flour.

A Legend

When crabs crawl up
out of the lake,

we tie them with ropes
and walk over the mountain
and stand by the pebbly road
of the market.

Some people eat crabs.

Hung up on ropes,
the crabs scratch the sky
with their ten hairy legs,
and are exchanged for money.
We buy a little rice and salt
and walk over the mountain
back to the shore of the lake.

Here
the grass is dead
and the wind is cold.
Our hut has no lights.

In the dark
we tell memories of our
    parents
to our children
over
and over again.
Our parents, too,
caught crabs, like us,
from this lake,
and walked over the mountain
to bring back a little rice and salt
to make hot gruel
for us children.

We, too, will soon go
as our parents did
to the lake
to dispose of
our withered little bodies
lightly,

lightly.
And crabs will eat up
our bodies completely,
just as they ate up
our parents' bodies
in times past.

This is our wish.

When our children have gone to
     sleep
we slip out of the hut
and row a boat out on the
     lake.
It is gray over the lake,
and trembling,
we make love
gently
and painfully.

Wild Duck

Did the wild duck say,
"Don't ever become a wild duck,"
at that time?

No.

We plucked the bird,
burned off its hair,
broiled its meat and devoured it,
and, licking our lips,
we began to leave the edge of the marsh
where an evening mist was hanging,
when we heard a voice:

"You could still chew
on my bones."

We looked back
and saw the laughter of the wild duck
and its backbone gleaming.

Takada Toshiko | (1914–1989)

TAKADA TOSHIKO was born in Tokyo and graduated from Atomi Girls' High School. She married in 1935, and went to Manchuria and lived in Harbin. When she returned with her family to Japan in 1946, she joined the Cotton Club, which later published *Gendai Shi Kenkyu* (*Studies of Modern Poetry*). Her first book of poems was *Sekka Sekko* (*Alabaster*, 1954). In the 1960s, Takada published poems in her column in the *Asahi* newspaper on Mondays. These were later collected into a volume, *Monday Poems*, which was warmly received by a broad public. She also started and edited a poetry magazine, *Nobi* (*Field Fire*), for women poets all over Japan in 1965. Her poems tell of the joys and sorrows of human life in clear, personable, and precise language.

The Fish

Someone, returning from Mexico,
brought me this gift of a fossil fish –
a fish with a pointed mouth like a *sayori* fish,
about six inches long, inlaid in rose-pink stone.
It's not a particularly unique fish,
but looks eerie because of its open, crushed eye.
The weird luster of its scales is frightening.
"Oh, how scary!" I was about to say and stopped.
The person only heard me say, "Oh."
He thought I was delighted and went home.
So I wrapped it in paper and put it away in the bookshelves,
its crushed eye watching me all the while.

But the look of the fish I'd seen would not vanish.
Heavy is the time that passed until it became a fossil.
Did the fish swim the seas of the glacial period?
It had swum through the ages and suddenly was there before me.
The anger contained in the crushed eye
of a fish, an ordinary small fish!

I too am an ordinary small fish.
In the blue light of midnight, as if led by the fish's eye,
I too begin to swim up the stream of time in the glacial sea.

The stream of time connecting the glacial period and now
is no more than the length of the Milky Way in the window frame
I used to gaze on as a child, lying in my bed before going to sleep.

The Beach

A boy riding on a horse
crosses the beach.

The horse's tail
sways along the horizon.

I pick up seashells and heap them on my breasts –
my grave.

Lying on the sand,
I smile.

Crimson Stone

In the infinite universe
on this drop of green
an accordion is playing,
and my fingers rest carefree
on your hands.

While light falls gently
on the breeze blowing over the treetops, torn by a shrike's scream,
the skin reddens
under my blouse, thinner than a cloud.

My heart, released from its torn outer cover,
embraces you –
the birth of a tender nymph.

Now we stop the tilting Earth
and plant an eternal prayer in one instant.

In the inner parts of our eyes, wet with mountain mist,
our souls seek each other's radiation.
Even the swaying hair and the turtledove's cooing seem
as if they are part of my breath.

I embrace the crimson stone
of the evening sun melting into woods.

Washisu Shigeo | (1915–1982)

WASHISU SHIGEO was born in Yokohama and baptized as an infant into the Greek Orthodox Church. He served in the army during the Sino–Japanese War and World War II. After the war he worked as a farmer in Hokkaido and then, in 1972, moved to Saitama, north of Tokyo. There he joined the Wan (The Bay) group and the Rekitei group. His poetry has an epic-like grandeur, owing to his extensive knowledge of Egyptian, Greek, and Latin mythology, plus the Old and New Testaments. A religious and metaphysical poet, he also has, in addition to his eight volumes of modern poetry, a collection of haiku and another of classical Chinese poems.

A Poet's Destiny

IN HONOR OF BORIS PASTERNAK

Always sticking your jaw out a bit,
you cast your gentle eyes on the white birches from the train
    rocking through the country.
The great Earth kept up the conversation with refined philosophy
    and rhythm
and played with the great pianist you loved.

In the dashing springtime, brilliant poetic lines were set free
from you. You were a fast-footed Arabian horse and you aged too
    soon.
Although you knew how heavy the weight of destiny is –
how a love of purity can exhaust an artist,
you were much too late in finding that out.

You heard somber thunderclaps on your deathbed –
whether in remembrance of the roaring boom of cannons, the
    soaring up of the Valkyrie,
or Francesca's plea for love, being carried along by the wind –

You often lost consciousness and fell like Dante.
On the day when your proud boots gathered a thin film of dust in
    the study,
modest people wept, burying your face in flowers.

Night in Assyria

This morning the birds stole the light and flew away.
An eruption far away. A coup d'état in the distance. A message
    flying over a blue lake.

This morning I saw a lame dog in the street during the snowstorm,
    the tears around its eyes frozen.
A train of cars loaded with gunpowder dashed by.
Then the shadows of pilgrims drifted past,
    singing.
The dark earth, evil dragons crawling about. Boris's usurpation
    and the anxieties.

Faithful night, shameless night, you will come around again
to the Virgin Mary and the Holy Infant, encircled by barbed wire.
Civilization is in the drawer. I take out and read some cards –
about Cicero's accusation, about the poison of Tacitus!
The tape recorder starts to turn. Lice crawl out of the mirror,
and their movement covers the world.

Again I am squeezed into a dark freight car in my dream.
A vicious cycle besets my pillow.
Where am I being taken? To Assyria, to Assyria!
The axles, as they chase the wheels, are singing
of the glory of the great Sargon of olden times,
of the expedition to the marine country, which would fail.
Like lumps of clay, the warriors keep the silence of the boundary
    stones.
    "Oh, you are inlaid into the relief of the night –
    of the night of one thousand years, carrying bows and
        arrows,
    with tense eyes, lining up solemnly on the edge of the wall
        of the sleepless gate.
    Pentagon, the winged king with the human face, takes tablets
        and is awake.
    Spiritual cow and ominous bird, you are to be buried in the
        ashes of ten thousand years,
    to be revived from the ashes of ten thousand years."

And you ashes, when will you again reveal in a shovelful of
    cinders
the writhing night, the wounded lions, the shadows of the yokes
    of the world which have gone reverberating by –
the head of the king of Edom hanged on a tree, the merry
    banquet –
the pile of discarded empty Coca Cola cans?

Again in a dream – in a dream I speak from the spiral staircase,
        from the weird ziggurat:
On Earth are the distorted bald heads of sleepless priests, and
    their mutterings:
    "Peter, the sand laughed at you.
    You are a passenger riding on an old street car, always
        returning from the last stop.
    Over the fence, stockings and a running cat can be seen."
    "A woman gets old when she finished singing a song.
    Peter, you stammer in the tavern, trying to preach."
    "Words exist among us like bitter enemies.
    Words float fondly in the evening sky like balloons."

This morning, for no reason, my dog disappeared.
And I see the warmth of a faint light tucked in the wings of a
    bird shot down for no reason.
This morning, I will again go out
to send off a telegram addressed to no one.

The Prayer of Judas Iscariot

1

Will the sun faithfully revolve over human beings forever? Or
will everything be absorbed into my death?
Will that beautiful person come to awaken my endless darkness?
Or will only the legend of a curious drama remain on the arid,
    dusty hill?

As I sold him to men, so he lends me to men.
Ah, how often did I visualize the sacrifice to the sacred ritual

of transfiguration,
the memory of sensing a wink somewhere, the dizziness of a boy on
    a summer day.
The sorrow of being the one chosen and its gravity – these will
    soon be weighed.

Now I have come, led by some invisible guide. People laugh at
    me.
Great Final Day of Judgment, you wait for something.
But I dislike a cumbersome procedure, not to mention an old-
    fashioned drama.
Therefore, be modest, you mere piece of rope – support me
    and be not arrogant.

2

My deed was heavier than the sack containing some silver,
and heavy was the time that passed through me.
I hear a horn in the distance. It is time that the sheep awake.
And I measure all sins.

Morning wind, my star watches over me,
looking at the extremity of my unhappiness from a distance
    farther than any constellation.
That person will suffer from the anguish of flesh torn apart.
He will think of love more deeply than I will hate myself.

There will be no end for me. He will be perfect.
But does he really know what is necessary for me, floating in the
    wind?
Does he know about the mere pinch of weight necessary to
    recognize myself clearly, not about love, not about hate?

Silver, let me be a unit of substance
so that I may weigh every sin, like you.
Star, let me be pure substance,
so that I may support every object there is, like you.

Ishihara Yoshiro | (1915–1977)

ISHIHARA YOSHIRO was born on Izu Peninsula in Shizuoka Prefecture. He graduated from Tokyo Foreign Language School in 1938, with a major in German. He studied Russian in the Japanese Army and was sent to Manchuria in 1941. Held as a "war criminal" by the Russians in Harbin, Manchuria, he was sentenced to twenty-five years of hard labor. After Stalin's death, he was granted amnesty and returned to Japan by way of Nakhodka in December 1953. He started to write poetry at the age of thirty-nine as a reaction to his internment and became a frequent contributor to the magazine *Arechi* during its final phase. His book of verse *Sancho Pansa no Kikyo* (*Sancho Panza's Homecoming*, 1963) won the fourteenth H-Shi Prize. Ishihara's poems seek to reconcile hope and resignation in a synthesis of acceptance. He employs modern postwar techniques with short, concise, but graceful lines. Besides poetry, he published a book about his life as a prisoner of war in Siberia, *Bokyo to Umi* (*The Longing for Home and the Sea*, 1972).

Wheat

Let a stalk of wheat
be your witness
to every difficult day.
Since it was a flame
before it was a plant,
since it was courage
before it was grain,
since it was determination
before it was growth,
and, above all, since it was prayer
before it was fruition,
it has nothing to point to
but the sky.
Remember the incredibly gentle wheat stalk
which holds its countless arrows fixed
to shoot from the bowstring –
you, standing in the same position
where the wind holds it.

The Accordion and Morning

I loved the accordion and morning.
I loved more than anything else
to see the morning fold
into the accordion
and scramble to get out
and turn into voices all sounding together.
I loved the accordion and night.
I loved more than anything else
to see the night lift the accordion
to its level
and then drop it
heavily.
I loved the accordion and death.
I loved them all through the night,
I loved them all through the morning.
When death played the accordion over and over,
the morning ended in the form of prayer.

The night ended in the form of prayer.

River

There is the mouth of the river.
That is where the river ends.
That is where the sea begins.
The river made sure of that place
and overflowed
and ran over it.
Riding over that place,
the river also produced the fertile riverbed.
It has defined its banks
with two streaks of intention
which cannot mix with the sea,
while the river itself keeps flowing
into the sea,
farther than the sea,
and more slowly than the sea.

Kuroda Saburo | (1919–1980)

KURODA SABURO was born in Kure City, Hiroshima Prefecture, but his family moved to Kagoshima City when he was three, and he lived there until he was twenty. Books by Nishiwaki Junzaburo and Haruyama Yukio fostered his interest in post-World War I Western literature. He joined the VOU group in 1936 and entered the Economics Department of Tokyo University in 1940. He went to Java in 1943, was recruited into the Army there in January 1945, and returned to Japan in 1946. Kuroda was a founder of the magazine *Arechi* with Tamura, Ayukawa, and others. His poetry uses plain, accessible language and draws on his daily life with sympathetic, humane perspectives. One of his books is a collection of poems about his life with his daughter, Yuri, while his wife was hospitalized.

Sleep, Neighbors

After an irritable day
comes the quiet night.
A large pale moon shines
on a roof from which a cat has gone.

Sleep, neighbors.
You, widow, who are so vain and stingy
and yet so easily flattered, sleep.
And you, broker, with your rimless glasses,
who talk in such a soft, unctuous voice on the phone, sleep.
And you, heavy-drinking carpenter, sleep.
Neighbors, sleep
after making your hubbub,
after working hard all day.

Shadow lies upon shadow.
Under
a large
pale moon
the world becomes one large shadow.
Dear neighbors, you have disappeared
into a shadow.
In the shadow
the vain widow dreams a dream;

the buttery-voiced broker dreams a dream;
the hard-drinking carpenter dreams a dream.

Weary from working through the night, I suddenly hear
the tormented sound of someone speaking out in their sleep.
In the wake of the ruthless interruption,
only irrevocable silence.

Strangely Fresh

it appears quite unexpectedly
from the depth of oblivion
like a lost object
that comes out
from under fallen leaves
piled up by winter winds –

the strangely fresh memory
of a moment of a day long gone by
why is it so?
what does it mean to me?
it is a simple thing
almost too simple a thing –

a deserted white country road in midsummer
which I saw from the train window traveling alone
the tune of someone's bright whistling I heard
on a station platform after an air raid
the faint scent of perfume
of a woman I passed by in the fog-filled valley of a night

Three O'clock on an Autumn Afternoon

Sitting on a bench by Shinobazu Pond
I secretly twist open the cap of my pocket whiskey flask.
In her new dress, my little daughter, Yuri,
runs straight out on the white sand
and comes back after drawing a circle there.

In the distance a sea lion raises its funny cry,
"*kwa, kwa, kwa.*"
Little Yuri comes back imitating the sea lion.
Three o'clock on an autumn afternoon.
Few people are around the flock of ducks on the opposite shore.

A car horn is heard faintly from far off.
Everything seems remote.
I see two shadows on the white sand
as in a distant, distant world,
shadows of an indolent father and his little girl.

Anzai Hitoshi | (1919–1994)

ANZAI HITOSHI was born in Fukuoka Prefecture and worked for the Fukuoka branch of the *Asahi* newspaper. In 1950 he moved to Tokyo to work for the Arts and Science section of the paper. There he joined the Rekitei group of Kusano Shinpei, the Chikyu group of Akiya Yutaka, and the Yama no Ki group of Ito Keiichi. Aside from books of poetry, he has written prose concerning poetry, notably *Watashi no Nihon Shishi Noto* (*My Notes on the History of Japanese Poetry*), *Sengo no Shi* (*Postwar Poetry*), and *Yasashii Shigaku* (*Easy Poetics*). Anzai was well-versed in classical Japanese literature and often uses allusions to the classics in his poems.

The Abandoned Horse

What on earth happened around here?
Where did it come from? Where did it go?
A wounded godlike warhorse was left behind and abandoned.
It stood for a while,
perplexed,
in the snow-covered field,
brighter than death,
more lonesome than freedom,
as helpless as peace.
The horse grazed a little on his own skinny shadow,
then raised a sudden neigh into the distance
and collapsed on his knees
under the evening sky, in the snowbound east.

The New Blade

My son is using a new razor
with clumsy hands.
Grooming himself as a grownup for the first time,
he spreads his elbows wide, as in a ritual,
very fastidiously, not looking sideways.
From below his temple a smear of blood
as big as a bird's tongue keeps flowing,
no matter how often he wipes it off,
and he looks a little afraid.

What is hurt in him, I wonder.
His naked back is moistened, shining bright
like a tree trunk with its bark peeled off.

Although he doesn't seem to hear them,
birds are singing loud in unison
around the young tree trunks.
He doesn't seem to see it,
but the sea is rolling in the mirror.

Confinement

I arrived at a certain town in the north
and confined my youth there one whole summer.
There were many hawks, kites, and crows in the town.
A flat rock had been lying asleep by the gate of a church.
I didn't know why it was put there,
but I was told that a crazed feudal lord
had an innocent pregnant women's belly cut open on it.
I waited for a little revelation, sitting on the legendary rock.
Every day, early in the afternoon, the old owner of the meat market
in front of the parsonage
threw a pinch of chopped meat on the street.
Then from somewhere in the hot, clear sky,
a hawk swooped down,
picked up the meat, and flew away.
The moment the hawk's claws snatched the meat
I thought I heard the slightest sound of the earth being touched,
and feeling the fleeting sensation over and over,
I endured the dull pain of the waste flesh of my youth being flayed off.

Yoshioka Minoru | (1919–1990)

Yoshioka Minoru was born in Honjo, Tokyo. He first wrote in the traditional forms of tanka and haiku but then turned to Western-style free verse. He studied in a commercial school at night but was drafted into the Army in 1940, and sent to Manchuria. He was on Cheju Island when the war ended. His book of poems *Soryo* (*Monks*), was published in 1958, and in 1959 he founded, with others, the magazine *Wani*. His earlier free verse reflects the influence of Kitasono Katsue and the art of Picasso. His poetry remained surreal, and his imagery was often abstracted and oblique. Yoshioka is one of the more difficult of the postwar poets to read, and one of the most highly praised.

A Hymn

I need to expand.
I long for the pleasant sound of water.
I find a portrait of a woman
in a room in the evening.
I am confused by its sensuality.
I try to be impressed in a different way.
Can't I prove the mixed functions of things?
In the corner of a very poor dining room
I contemplate
the death of the woman.
For the first time the woman somehow has died in me.
The eyes of the woman in the portrait move
away from the frame.
The stars that were shining
in her hair
are now fogged and out of position.
When all humankind has gone to sleep from the world of cruel reality,
I look for a new world,
a nail of dawn
in the loop at the end of the rope.
The plentiful fruits of autumn
are definitely moving closer to the reflected sky.
My hunger,
my thirst appear.
The lamp of the morning crawls on the ground,

and an egg is on the table, displaying its freshness.
Unacknowledged by anyone,
my purity vibrates.
Going over fires, rivers and human beings,
shaking off drops of dew from my whole body,
gallantly, drastically,
I transform myself
into a young beast that devours the egg.

In Praise of the Aged

An old man is accompanied
by a lonely, naked infant and a pelican.
He saws down all the trees in the woods
that would confirm the virtue of the flesh and the isolation of the mind
for the time of his death as king of the unwell,
and builds a phantom ship
as slowly as he can.
I saw it from under a nightgown.
All that is loaded aboard are broken teeth.
From his homeland of hemorrhoids and consumption
the old man sets out.
He rides over the surges that swell from under the skin,
setting his hairy wife on her face.
From the poison of black breasts
one's mind is badly disturbed
and even the body of a jellyfish is dark.
The old man laughs heartily.
Banzai.
Banzai.
Since even dying is a new experience, undergone for the first time,
on the night when he crosses the border with its broken hinges,
the bellies of the fish that cannot be torn apart shine continuously,
ceaselessly contracting,
exerting tremendous pressure, as well,
and looking erotic,
thus keeping the polite old man from sleeping.
Under the lusciousness of the gauzy moon
the old man reminisces.

To be exact, he creates,
for the stomach and bladder,
nights in the desert without a change of shift,
cries of hyenas and vultures,
markets where stars and sand are equal.
Sitting in the center of flames in a hut,
he tries to boil brightly-colored blood
in the vessel of a king's heart.
He is like a bamboo basket
laid uselessly upside down.
In the unquiet world of hair
where no fine naked dancer appears,
the master of the barbershop brandishes his razor,
shaving off the old man's full head of hair.
He is as cold as plaster.
As a perfect dead person
and as guardian deity of the infant and the pelican,
he is moved to a place
where he will not get in the way of others.

A Picture of Dry Matrimony

Both flowers and pistols are
soon buried under dead leaves,
and like calendars
slip into the funeral procession.
Dreams cool off on the plate.
The wedding of the night on an upper floor
looks gorgeous
only in the woman's hand mirror.
From the basin of distilled water,
which is held by the auctioneer,
men spill down silently
into a deserted garden
and soon dry up.

So Sakon | (1919–)

So Sakon was born in Fukuoka Prefecture. He studied philosophy at Tokyo University, where he developed special interest in Rimbaud and Valéry. The influence of French symbolists and surrealists is evident throughout his work. He lost his mother in the confusion and horror of an air raid on the night of May 25, 1945. This tragic experience is hauntingly recorded in a long narrative poem, *Moeru Haha* (*Mother on Fire*, 1967), which holds a unique place in the postwar poetry of Japan. So Sakon is also a novelist and art critic.

Grandma

Grandma,
you innocently smiling grandma,
lured by the swirl of lively, bursting laughter
from your son, born of your womb,
from your daughter-in-law, from your grandchildren born of them,
you smile as brightly as a baby
outside the house as old as your bent back;
Grandma,
it's a lovely day for winter, isn't it?
Doggie, too, the eleventh member of your family,
who cannot be unchained, comes up to the porch with its ears alert.
The sunny spot bubbles with warmth, giving off a scent like soap,
but Doggie's eyes are drawn off to the distant sky.
What is it that's glistening there, I wonder.
Is it the crest of a cloud crumbling like an avalanche
or a shadow of the dizzily rotating Earth?
Anyway, it is something too blinding to see, thus invisible,
so Doggie is trying to raise a growl peering at it.
Grandma,
you are smiling gently at the frightened look in Doggie's eyes.
Having given birth to so many futures,
those of your son, your daughter-in-law, and your grandchildren born of them,
your big mother body sends out strong ripples of gentle light.
You have sunk all the sorrow, anguish, and pain to the bottom, making them all
transparent,
you are the newest member of the family, born when you no longer could bear
a child.

You are your own baby.
You smiling grandma,
smiling, glad about being able to communicate with Doggie without words.
Seen from a spaceship,
the Earth is a mere blue lemon.
We, your children and grandchildren, may fly off
to an entirely new heavenly body with the speed of a spaceship,
leaving you and Doggie on this sunny spot,
but even then you would be the center of the light
which could change that lump of stone floating in space,
far beyond the distant sky Doggie is peering at,
into a dreamlike lemon
with the ripples of your innocent smiles –
Grandma.

Music in Winter

Even with the brand-new curtain drawn aside
the sky no longer enters through the window.

At the end of the naked tree's twig, the bird suddenly is motionless,
pierced by the icicle of its yesterday's voice.

In the dug-up deposit of tomorrow's crystal,
the minnow becomes a transparent regret with its eyes open, fossilized.

The night has soaked into the bottom of the Earth and never comes back.
Noontime exists only for the wings of the plane plunging into the sea.

In the broken compact mirror that cannot fly apart,
a cigarette, unsmoked, raises a wisp of crimson smoke.

The man keeps looking at the soup plate that remains unfilled.
The sound of the fish's fins gasping at the bottom of the plate raises no bubble.

The unwet glance never reaches the dry lips,
and the pot cracks at the blue edge of darkness that turns into fruit.

Youth, music in winter, the brightness on my gallows.

Even if the sky tries to enter the room through the window,
the brand-new light is now frozen like the curtain.

The Earth

The rocket was blasting away.
Green apples were swaying.

The void was blowing up reality.
Through the silver sky a snake went flowing by.

The rocket was blasting.
While blasting, it stayed motionless.

Stars were scattering over the ground.
Jewels were dreaming with their eyes closed.

The Earth fell in the garden of a future morning.
The rocket, unable to fly, kept blasting.

Nakagiri Masao | (1919–1983)

NAKAGIRI MASAO was born in Fukuoka Prefecture and lived in Kobe. In 1937, he started the magazine *LUNA*, the name of which, owing to the government's anti-Western language policy, had to be changed to *Shishu* (*Anthology*). In 1939, he entered the Department of Arts at Nihon University. Though he served in the Japanese Army and wrote some war poems, he had not experienced military action, having been discharged for ill health. He worked as a newspaper reporter from 1945 to 1968, and became a lecturer in English literature at Hosei University. An early leader in contemporary poetry, he was prominent among those who started up the postwar magazine *Arechi*. Nakagiri also translated poetry by W. H. Auden, Stephen Spender, and C. Day Lewis. His Japanese translation of Auden is especially well regarded.

Thanatopsis

Don't talk about death with others.
Don't speak the word which vanishes like smoke.
You can't see death.
What is there at that moment is nothing but ashes.
Death is the light of the sun.
Death is today.

Don't live today by means of tomorrow.
Don't ever say, "But tomorrow I will...."
Your fate will be cut down
as easily as weeds by the roadside,
but don't try to avoid it,
try rather to promote it.

Ants' lives,
the life of green mold,
lives of the fish in the sea,
a piece of ruby,
the hair of a rose engraved in stone.

Huge things are still sham.
Even a little knowledge can witness everything.
Cut off your ears.

Burn out your eyes.
Let your thin heart endure
the pain of learning everything.

Lie down in mud.
Cover yourself with decayed leaves.
Let your cheeks shiver.
Let your blood drip, and accept the rain
with all your body.
Assimilate mercy.

A Poem for New Year's Eve

The final night,
the dark time headed for the first day,
the night alive with silent snow falling,
with animals far away.
This night is formed
in the midst of things uncertain
in everything cold and pathetic.

Petty misery taps on the windowpane
and human eyes glisten in the sorrow of ashes.
The last song hangs over the earth,
and in the dark
the holy moment is slowly drawing near –
the moment when death and life lie on top of each other.
Is there anything left for us to do
before the tiny dot in Time leaps upon us?

Oh, the holy moment.
We are told only
that all the great words have already been spoken,
that even the promise of life is but another form
of the promise of death.
Oh, the holy moment.
Through the door opened for tomorrow
all the future flows in
and the room glows with the glint of crystal and darkness.

Oh, the holy moment.
I forget and am forgotten.
As a corpse falls into the grave
I fall into my self,
into my narrow, dark channel,
into my dark tomorrow.

At Night

I am always smiling.
I smile at everyone,
as if I had forgotten how to get mad,
as if it were my fate to smile,
but really,
I sell my god every night.

My body is full and voluptuous,
my hair is rich and black,
I am always warm,
always satisfied,
and I always smell good.
But when I stand under the elevated railway
with a cigarette in my mouth,
my sinfulness becomes as real
as the sun.

I receive a death sentence every night.
What good is there in the beauty of a criminal sentenced to death?
Repeated sinning by a criminal under the death sentence
is like a dot added to infinity, isn't it?
I pucker up my mouth
and blow cigarette smoke in the men's faces.
A cargo train goes across my mind
making unpleasant grating sounds.
Am I the only one experiencing this?

Ah, I want so terribly much to get mad.
At least, I want to tell myself
that even a criminal under a death sentence has the right to get mad.

"There is no pleasure, no matter how refined,
that can't be reduced to prostitution."
A French poet said that.

Sekine Hiroshi | (1920–1994)

SEKINE HIROSHI was born in the Asakusa section of Tokyo. He began to work to earn a living upon finishing primary school in 1932. In 1940 he joined the Bunka Soshiki (Cultural Organization) with Ono Tozaburo and others, and took part in left-wing democratic movements, which had been suppressed in the 1930s. He worked as a journalist from 1939 to 1958, but devoted his time and talent thereafter to writing as a poet and critic, his viewpoint being consistently socialistic. Sekine was active in various literary movements and played a leading role in the Retto group and the Gendaishi group. His writing is versatile and includes reportage, social criticism, literary criticism, novels, and plays.

The Child and the Birds

The child likes things that move,
things big enough to ride on:
streetcars, automobiles,
the swing in the park.
He likes small things that quiver:
birds in a bird store,
goldfish in a goldfish store.
He likes things that flicker:
the neon signs.

He likes rhythmic movement.
He likes to watch the fingers
that move
over a silent piano keyboard
on the TV screen with the sound off.

The child who is friendly with birds can see
voiceless voices,
soundless songs,
and time yet to come.

A Serenade

Tapping me on the back, the night says,
"Don't stay home.
Go look for what you lost yesterday."
What I lost yesterday
resembles what I had lost the day before yesterday,
and what I lost the day before yesterday
resembles what I had lost the day before that:

the backside of the board slipping down perpetually;
something that vanishes each time I go looking for it;
the nightly thirst while I'm walking along roads full of chuckholes,
carrying an empty bag.

Perhaps it is something small.
Perhaps it is visible, perhaps invisible.
Perhaps it is something like a right.

I dream that the bag is too heavy for me to carry,
and when weightless morning comes I do it all over again.
Today I found
an utter stranger looking
for the same article that I had lost.

Moving Out of the Room

I am moving out of this room,
leaving behind my yardstick of time.

I have taken out my books.
I have taken out the desk.
I have taken out my clothes.
I have taken out other various junk.
I have also taken out love.

I am leaving in it
the obsolete foot warmer,
charcoal brazier, and such.

But of course what makes me feel sad
is not these things.
I am sad because I am leaving behind
a load of memories not even a large truck could carry.

I am leaving all the memories
in the empty room.
But I will surely come back
to get them,
you know, landlord!

Ishigaki Rin | (1920–)

ISHIGAKI RIN was born in Akasaka, Tokyo. She began work at a bank as soon as she finished primary school and stayed at that job for forty-one years, taking part in union activities. She published her poems in the union newsletter, where they were read and admired by Ono Tozaburo and Yamamoto Taro. One of the best known women poets in Japan, she belongs to the Rekitei group. Her poetry displays its common touch through the use of simple language and the viewpoint of a working woman, yet her imagery is often surprisingly powerful.

Hands

My outspread hands,
the hands in front of me.
These are alive,
alive and moving.

These hands some day will be old.
These hands some day will stop moving.

They will be folded by the hands of others who will mourn over me,
will be placed on my cold chest,
and stay for a while
in the world where my soul will no longer exist.
Ah, when the outside world is filled with light
and a soft breeze blows just like today,
what will the dry skin of these hands see and feel
for the eyes
that are closed?

Hands,
where will you dispose of
all the memories
of the many things you have held?
Tell me.
    (When I look away,
    I see a procession of many creatures
    moving away one after another

waving their hands like flower petals.
Where are they going?)

Unmistakably, these are the expressions of my hands,
vivid and sad,
of the living hands of my mortal self.

When I put my hands together, they feel strangely warm,
giving me a singular sense,
certain but imperceptible,
that they are mine
and that some day they will be gone.

These Days

My breasts feel full and heavy in both my hands
like the sea filled with its last flowing tide.

Apples are good for plucking now.
Mackerel pike are good in autumn,
glistening bright, fat, good to eat.
   (Suddenly I come to myself and am surprised
   at my own warm body.)

This is life at its height,
given to living creatures that perish in time.

It is the sole season given to mortal beings
who will soon die and fall
just like the wind rustling in the trees,
just like the dew shining on the flowers.

In this beautiful sunlight
how will the flowers fall?
And how will the trees bear fruit?
I think about preparations for perishing
with a restless heart these days....

An Island

I stand in the large full-length mirror,
a tiny island,
quite alone,
isolated from everyone else.

I know
the history of the island,
its size,
its waist, bust, and hips,
its dress for each of the four seasons,
its warbling birds,
its hidden fountain,
and the scents of its flowers.

I live
on my island,
plowing and building,
but I cannot know everything
about this island,
nor can I live permanently here.

In the mirror I stare at myself –
a distant island.

Kisaragi Shin | (1920–)

Kisaragi Shin was born in Kagawa Prefecture. He was affiliated early with the magazine LUNA, edited by Nakagiri Masao, which later became LE BAL and then *Shisu* (*Anthology*), and joined the Arechi group after the end of World War II. He lives in his hometown in Kagawa Prefecture, in northeastern Shikoku, which is bounded on three sides by the Inland Sea, a location often reflected in his poetry.

A Song of the Flying Fish

It lives a life bluer than a surge below surges.
The bone as supple as a filament
bends with pliable flesh made of plankton and tides.
It sinks swiftly like a shot lead bullet.

Splashing, it rejects the seagull's plaintive cries.
Filling a violent wind in its pectoral fins,

it pauses for a moment in the dangerous air.
Its passage doesn't reach a star – a spindle-shaped misfortune.

Packing cries in its moist white chest,
its side glistens in the sun like a spent candle.

It is used to being chased, chased, always chased
like a pierced lie.
When it dies, it has no blood, no fat.

The Typhoon

Madly sliding down a cliff of clouds
the winds
break the crests of the waves
and seize the land.
In their too violent embrace
the sea is torn apart.
Under the furious blows of the waves
the body of summer's love is washed ashore.

It catches on the crevice of the breakwater with its claws,
but the tide is at its ebb now.
Pushed by the winds,
pulled by the moon,
confused, the force of the waves
trembles.
The voice, blown and broken from the heaven of memory,
falls groaning somewhere in the invisible night.

About Time

When a butterfly is pinned down, a stream of time stops.
But that is not all. Like a mountain stream

going around a rock, the other stream of time flows on.
Time can travel fast or slow, narrow or broad.

An invisible voice urges, "Hurry up ... hurry up ... hurry up ..."
But everything depends on the topography.

Mathematics assumes time travels at a uniform speed. So,
mathematics is wrong. Time

can travel fast or slow. When mathematics comes into play
everything goes amiss.

A length of time can be measured with a clock,
but its speed cannot be measured. When the war in the film

being projected stops, a comedian shows his face
from a corner. At that point, time stops.

When news is written down in pencil on rough paper,
news dies.

When the rotary press stops,
it revives.

"The dead one is young forever," believes
the poor mother by herself. Sea with floating seaweed

moistens her monologue.
Time begins to flow torrentially like teardrops.

There's truth in the monologue, but time has nothing to do with sentiment
It flows around the rock. Nothing can be done to topography.

Ayukawa Nobuo | (1920–1986)

AYUKAWA NOBUO, a native of Tokyo, joined Nakagiri Masao's LUNA magazine in 1937. He left to join the army during his junior year at Waseda University, where he was majoring in English, and was sent to Sumatra. He returned to Japan in 1944, due to illness. Ayukawa holds an important position among postwar poets as one of the central figures in the Arechi group that opened a new, fertile field for free-verse lyrics in mid-twentieth century Japanese poetry. Since his death a ten-volume edition of his writings has been published by Shicho-sha.

After the Summer

1
a cold sea wind
blows on a cold mirror

2
the sky is blue and high and far
the seagulls perhaps
find their own shadows on the broken rocks

3
leaving a lonely smile behind
a woman has left without saying goodbye
soon the waves will attack
and wash away the figure of a man from the shore

4
I will throw away every dream I have
life is a walking shadow
a footprint on crumbling sands
the white bone
of a fish which has died, caught by the shore

5
a white sail floats far off

The Rotation of Non-Desire

1

Blood jets out
toward the light of the stars.
Where the sea reverberates through a dark tunnel
a seashell twists itself in the flowing water.
A pine tree grows old. Behind an anchor,
a solitary fish lives.
When these things were part of the history of ships
the sea was dark, the cliffs were white.

2

During the daytime
one seeks gratification of desire within the movement of the sun;
and where the hands and feet quietly bend
like hair,
the blood, without eyes, without ears, just keeps on flowing,
moistening the tongue of the desert
like blue rain, like a swallow.
Flowers spread their ancient roots
and grow thick, raising flames.
From inside the window of their burning world
they look out at a sphere without horizon, without smoke,
and see the tentacles of reeds, rustling slightly.
In the room a dim-lit lantern
engraves a motionless head.
It is a serpent drowsing
in a golden vessel
like the legend of progress in medical science.

3

A bush warbler lays eggs in the hair
of you who are dreaming this dream.
Your brains turn pale as poison.
The clock is softly twisted.
A green stalk stuck in a vase
decorates a hyacinth's neck.
Its ascending stairway is surrounded
by clouds that leap up like springs.

On the heavy neck
that moves through the mottled bright light,
hiding in the shade, wearing a white collar,
a hot wind comes down
like a piece of lead.
A waxen match laughs.
In the transparent sap of the trees
great numbers of bush warblers close their eyes.
Underneath their harp
a purple glove has thrown
the seeds of apples.
Goodbye, goodbye, bad memory
of the long afternoon nap.
Goodbye.

4
On a tree hangs a body.
The shadow of death is magnified.
On a barren map
towers a white building.
While prayerless cries
and toothless laughter fight each other
constantly,
the mysterious spinning wheel
keeps turning with a murmur.
On a clear morning, when the key to the cemetery is delivered,
the pale body
takes off its skin, which has withered with desire,
and climbs up the ladder.

A Room

The window washes the room blue
with bright seawater.
The flower does not see the creature that has eyes.
The tilted desk does not hear the wind.
Ah, gentle stalk,
fastened with rusty thumbtacks,
you have vanished in the veins of the navigator's chart.

Ah, transparent green,
no one knows of the small jewel box
nor of the delivered papers on the stone floor.
Was it last year's song that brushed
past the tree's shadow? It's no longer there.
A hat that smells of a seashell
is asleep in the mirror.
Only the clock is awake.
Even when it strikes twelve,
the chairs sit empty
and the dead people live in the wall
on white sand.

Miyoshi Toyoichiro | (1920–1992)

MIYOSHI TOYOICHIRO was born in Hachioji, west of Tokyo. Owing to poor health, he was not drafted ino the army during World War II. He worked for a camera manufacturing company in a suburb of Tokyo, where he privately published a magazine, *Koen* (*An Old Garden*). When it was discontinued after only three issues, he put out three more issues using mimeograph printing. Together with Ayukawa, Nakagiri, Tamura, and Kitamura, Miyoshi was one of the founders of the *Arechi* magazine. His first book, *Shujin* (*The Prisoner*), published in 1949 and generally considered the first significant book in postwar Japanese poetry, expressed the sense of darkness and despair in Japan during and right after the war. The first two selections in this anthology are taken from *Shujin*.

Shadow 1

The sound of shoes going down to the grave in the dark
tremulously, endlessly.
Lonely dialogue from downstairs, like prayer, like repentance.
It suddenly ceases.
I put on the light. So that the dark cannot steal me away,
I only let the light spread out around me
and begin to smoke, hoping for a little pleasure at least.
An unshaven, hollow-cheeked, sorrowful, yet familiar face
stares at me from behind the cold darkness beyond.
A lonely lord –
my small, round territory expands with the glow!
I put out the light and I fall.
I lose myself, and in the dark, as if groping for black death,
I touch someone's face.

The Blue Tavern

At the tip of my left lung is a hole eaten by a worm.
When I lie quietly, closing my eyes, I can hear through the hole
someone sipping liqueur from a glass at a blue tavern, in winter,
together with the sound of a biting cold wind blowing over great distance.
The thin little man with a guitar is all by himself
with his back to the wall late at night.

There is no one to talk to.
All that blows in with the wind is freezing regret.

The man now twangs the strings of his hoarse guitar
and now tilts his head uneasily. When he gets tired
even of looking at his own emaciated face in the glass,
he busily wipes the table.

A dog, while no one was looking, has sneaked into
the man's shadow on the floor, to live there
and grow fat, feeding on the man's unmanageable despair.
He is such an intolerable thing.
Through the hole eaten by the worm in my chest
I can hear his painful coughing. Yet in the daytime
I neatly put on my coat and vest and walk in the street,
like an optimist.
Every night I see him again at the blue tavern.
He has aged as much as I, but he isn't about to die yet.
From time to time, he smiles slyly.

Shadowgraph

At that time, since the sand will burst into flames,
birds pushing their way through the light would be branded
on the wall of the sky in the exact shape of their flight.

At that time, the beasts running around in the scorching sun
looking for water in dried-up river beds
will be moving stains on the earth, like ants on stampede.

At that time, the wings of flame beating on the entrails
will nail up red flowers of sore flesh
in the broken doorways, like scars from the plague.

At that time, the sun, like a crouching hag with her tangled hair
wearing a mourning dress of black smoke,
will become the obsession of the hapless universe.

At that time, the cries of children, scratching at space,
making their thin, sharp nail marks on it,
will draw a vivid sketch of a shrieking woman.

At that time, standing at the end of the yellow horizon,
a man staring with his sightless eyes
will be only a rusty steel skeleton or a bitter metaphysical idol.

At that time, nothing will belong to this world any more.
Oh hungry bones, rotten flesh, senseless objects;
oh anguish of the future, in the darkness I see them all.

Naka Taro | (1922–)

NAKA TARO was born in Fukuoka City, and studied Japanese literature at Tokyo University. Drafted into the Japanese Navy, he taught Japanese at the Naval Academy of Japan until the end of World War II. His first book of poetry, *Etudes* (1950), shows the influence of Paul Valéry (1871–1945) and Hagiwara Sakutaro (1886–1942). In his second book, *Ongaku* (*Music*), he created his distinctive "distilled" language. Japanese poets seldom employ alliteration or rhyme purposively, but Naka Taro is an exception, skillfully combining consonants and vowels in his use of Japanese sounds.

The Candle

Like the darkness spreading behind the light,
a void lurks at the base of everything,
and, just as a point of light is supported by the darkness itself,
isn't it the void itself that gives meaning to all existence?

Oh, candle, you who take fire onto yourself to burn out,
everything exists only to perish. For this reason alone,
isn't everything infinitely beautiful?
Since resistence to dying makes one conscious of life,

who can say that your flickering flame is meaningless waste?
Alone in the room, deep at night, I peer at you.
You burn away your life, giving off light,
faintly swaying your wick.

Your inner life condenses itself into a small ring of light,
and lights up the world all around –
the desk, the vase, the door, and the eyes – whatever you light up –
they, in turn, lean intensely toward you.

Should I say they are witnesses to your existence?
Or should I say you are the witness to all of them?
White wax, you keep burning yourself, wavering.
Like painful prayer, your flame glows white to calm itself.

Ah you – essence that overflows from within!
What can time ever detract from you?
You keep alive only by ceaselessly destroying yourself.

Thus your wick condenses itself into a sharp needle,
and like a shaft of ice that rips an abyss,
your light shines brightly, breaking forth from the darkness.

Decalcomania II

poetry is the glitter of needles scattered on marble
the eye is a magnet that converges the light

death is the transparent sap that rises through the tree
the bud is a thorn that is nurtured by it and stings the outside world

*

poetry is the shadow of a bird that has flown away
the eye is a bullet that follows its flight

death is the rioting of a moth round the crown of night
the bud is the flame that settles on a candlestand

*

poetry is a black rose
the eye is a trembling tentacle

death is seaweed in disarray at the bottom of the sea
the bud is a blade that cuts

*

poetry and death are codes:
the eye and the bud decode them

poetry and death are pollen:
the bud and the eye carry them away.

NOTE: The words "poetry" and "death" are both pronounced *shi* in Japanese, and
    "eye" and "bud" are both pronounced *me*.

Cityscape

In the hushed street
there is no dry sound of shoes passing by like shadows
on the pavement.
The houses standing side-by-side have their shutters down.

Where have all the dead leaves that used to rustle in the golden dust gone?
Where has the pale face of the sick, gaunt woman
who used to look outside all day from the second-floor balcony gone?

The doors of the brown buildings remain nailed shut.
Bleakly, the bones of the tree branches touch the air.

God, no one calls your honorable name any more.

The sea spreads wide over the zinc roofs,
and an invisible flag flutters briskly on a spire.

Kihara Koichi | (1922–1979)

KIHARA KOICHI was born in Tokyo. At age fifteen he joined the avant-garde magazine *vou* group led by Kitasono Katsue. He worked for the Japanese Army as a construction engineer in China and Iwo Jima and returned to Japan just before the U.S. forces landed on the island. After the war he joined the Arechi group and wrote of the cruelty and misery of war. Later he became known for his lyric poems, such as the selections in this anthology, and his prizewinning radio plays.

Where Do You Come From?

where do you come from?

out of a blind stone
out of the folded petals of an unopened rosebud

where are you?

in front of a mirror that reflects dying people
in front of a mirror that reflects those being born

where will you go?

to a height that even fluttering birds cannot reach
to a depth that even fish in the sea cannot plumb

The Knocking at the Door

Listen, in your heart,
to that which is knocking at the door,
to that which awakens a sleeping snake! It
    makes an eternal virgin pregnant,
    and it offers a kingdom   to those who seek.
    In it   a voice changes   into a distant echo.

Look at it in life!
that which drops on the desert,
that which makes a stung wasp come back to life! It

is a suspension bridge spanning the river from one bank to the
    other.
It is the past   in a mirror that reflects the future.
In it, the eye sees a bottomless chasm.

Catch it in death,
that which gives light to the stars,
that which makes a blind fish swim. It
    is a seed   that a dying person has sown.
    It is a straw   that a newborn has grasped for.
    In it, the ear meets the Time we have never met.

Small Bridges

Since the very day that I was born
I have been learning only this:
to build bridges in the world   as many bridges as I can.

Against the morning light
I build a bridge across the narrow space between two buildings.
I build a bridge over the gap   between the hearts
of people who aimlessly rush by,
but
no one's hand can connect the distance
between hearts that are torn apart.

Under the infrared rays of the evening
I build a bridge between the passing moment and the upcoming
    moment.
I build a bridge betwen the love and hatred of a person
who is walking with his head drooping, without reason.
And I dream of completing a bridge someday
between human and human, between time and place
which no storms can destroy.

Ever since the very moment I was born
I have lived with only this thought:
to build bridges in the world   as many bridges as I can.

Kiyooka Takayuki | (1922–)

KIYOOKA TAKAYUKI was born in Dairen in former Manchuria and studied French literature at Tokyo University. He once worked for the Japan Federation of Professional Baseball as planner of game schedules. He published his early poetry in the *Wani* (*Crocodile*) magazine. In his poetry he writes of his daily experiences, of dreams, and of nature, with fresh imagery and exceptional lucidity. He translated the poetry of Rimbaud into Japanese (1968) and, with Ooka Makoto and Inoue Yasushi, edited a collection of French translations, *Anthologie de poésie japonaise contemporaine* (Gallimard, 1986). Kiyooka also writes novels and criticism.

The Man Playing the Oboe

(LISTENING TO THE LEIPZIG GEWANDTHAUS ORCHESTRA)

Each member of the orchestra on TV
quite abruptly commits his wings
to the breeze of a rest, and silently
keeps gliding for a moment
through the sky of the symphony.
They have come carrying their instruments from Germany,
bearing the air of migratory birds.
Tonight my tired body slips refreshed and pleased,
into the depths of their momentary silence,
fully released
from the trials of a man
who couldn't help working with all his heart by day,
even in a miserable job.
The TV screen is now showing
a close-up of an honest-looking oboe player
who is sucking in his cheeks.
I am sniffing
at the smell of a strange land and roses
in the slow flow of quiet time;
and I am wondering absently
what that thin-haired man with the slightly bulging eyes
is thinking of life.

Midsummer

Two o'clock in the afternoon.
New business once again
chases me
out of the air-conditioned office on the seventh floor
down to the car on the hot street of baking asphalt.
My re-tightened snakeskin belt gives a playful whip
to my body, which, more than anyone's, I know,
is sensitive to heat.
In the automatic elevator,
forgetting everything but my destination,
I become the forefinger of my right hand
and push the button for the first floor,
lighting up the light like a firefly.
The fan overhead blows and cools only my hair,
and then I turn into just two legs
supporting a downward dizziness.

A rectangular box with its parallel lines,
about the size of a telephone booth,
moving up and down –
is it like a prison cell?
Is it like a womb?
Or:
Is it like an upright coffin?
In the middle of the overcrowded city, in broad daylight,
I am completely secluded from everyone else
in this suddenly secret room.

In its mysterious freedom
I have nothing to think of.
At the same time
I am rather nervous about myself,
being unable to think about anything.
The world is far away and vague,
and my heart seems languid and guilty.
Oh, how many times have I felt
this futile self-consciousness?
Oh, I want to go to the sea!

In the flash of these thoughts
there is the distant echo
of the change of seasons, as
the elevator comes to a stop,
the door silently opens, and
my twenty-four-second solitude is over.

The Length of One Day

Oh, how short a fine spring
holiday can be!
I finally awoke at noon
as if crawling out of a week-long fatigue.
At the bottom of the soup I had for brunch
was a quail's egg –
a small part of the mystery
that would sustain my heart through the day.
And now it is night already.
The day is gone
and what have I done?
I wrote some postcards in reply to unanswered letters
and while I was out to mail them
I took a walk
and stopped in a store
and looked at a bathtub, thinking I might replace my old one,
and came home, and after supper
I listened, spellbound for a while,
to the hectic play of strings
which sounded like the winds blowing
off the seventeenth-century Mediterranean.
What else did I do?
The child is sound asleep
with his knapsack ready for school tomorrow.
As I quietly bend and touch the child's hair with my cheek
it smells of warm sunshine,
it smells of sand, grass, pigeons, dogs, and building blocks,
and it smells of almost sweet perspiration.
The time of growing is ever slow.
How deep is the world of children where dreams are mingled,
and how long a day can be!

Nakai Hideo | (1922–1993)

NAKAI HIDEO was born in Tokyo and studied in the Department of Linguistics of Tokyo University. He began his poetry career as editor of tanka magazines, *Nihon Tanka*, *Tanka Kenkyu*, and *Tanka*, for twelve years and has written a book about editing these magazines. His own poems are short and concise, notable for their use of many colors. Nakai is also known as a fiction writer with books of mystery, fantasy, and short stories.

Music

while alive
I never knew
that what I touched
was such a gentle song

only my ear knew
and now
only my ear remembers

that I was once alive
and that once
I even felt it
with my fingers

The White Dog

A white dog appears quite casually
at the foot of the tree in my yard,
dragging along a silver chain
in the rain falling in the darkness.
When he turns, his eyes are full of curses and loneliness,
looking as if he had been there for years.

While I am writing under the bright light,
his chain clanks and grates.
When I take notice of him,
he disappears into the falling rain,

leaving behind his eyes, full of loneliness.
I don't know what he comes here for.
It is just a white dog that comes to the tree in my yard every night.
It is a white dog full of loneliness and curses.

Larme Noire

Poetry has been
my black tears.
As I shed them,
they stained my cheeks.
For such a long time,
poetry has been
my black tears –
truly black tears.
But now poetry has run its course.
If I should shed anything now,
it would be blood, even from my eyes.
I will no longer shed anything
but blood.

Akiya Yutaka | (1922–)

AKIYA YUTAKA was born in Saitama Prefecture. He was a student at Nihon University when he was drafted into the Japanese Navy and served in the South Pacific. Much of his poetry is based on his war experiences. As an advocate of "neo-romanticism," he founded the poetry magazine *Chikyu* (*The Earth*) in 1950, which published its 100th issue in 1991. Noted as a socially-conscious lyric poet, Akiya is also known for climbing the Himalayas and many Japanese mountains, along with a book he wrote about mountain climbing. His 1991 volume of poetry is *Haikyo to Yamagutsu* (*Ruins and Mountain Boots*).

Fairy Tale of the Mountains

The sound of the evening breeze
coming from distant mountains
stirs a lonely evening primrose
blooming silently
far up in the grass of the highlands.

The colts noisily call
each other
out of the shade of woods and grass.
They romp home in high spirits today
as always, heartily neighing to each other.

The reason why the smell of pollen
drifts in the dusk
gently hovering over the pasture
must be because they have run
all over the highlands.

Soon, when night falls over the highlands
and the moon rises like a hanging lamp,
the colts, tired out, will sleep fast,
and the lone evening primrose
will sway in a dream.

Bloodshed

Today's sun shines on my wound
in broad daylight.
In the afternoon bed, perspiration dries
and I sleep with a stone in my arms.
I sleep like a torso
with its arms melted
in the dark sunlight:

It's noon now. A towering cumulus cloud flares nearby,
and I can let even
my memory of the nightmare bleed:
An unfamiliar soldier moves slowly
out of the yellow rapeseed flowers
holding a rifle.
In the sharp aim of his eyes
a bird is set.

Fireworks of thought exploding in a white sky
with a heavy metallic sound
suddenly cut off my arm.
Next to my prostrate head,
vainly blowing up the quivering petals of melancholy
and the fossil of burning civilization,
the bird falls!

The pitiable blood shed in the summer grass
somewhere west of Mandalay – oh, how vain –
now rises from the wound in my arm
through the wilderness inside
like tree sap flowing;
but my wounded form can no longer
hold my loved one,
my wounded fingers can no longer strum
the lonely instrument.

Today's sun is about to leave
with its daylight.
Putting on the light in my closed room,

I enter quietly
into the yellow rapeseed flowers again.
I am a bird asleep.
Ahead of me, only the branches of trees
in the distant night glimmer.

North Country

In the depth of rustling windbreak forests
pale fog is frozen
in the eyes of a wild duck shot down.

I finish writing my dismal personal history,
soaked in the cool light of the lamp.

All night long the wild duck, not quite dead,
beats its wings in the dry grass,
and I only keep tossing in my bed.

Kitamura Taro | (1922–1992)

KITAMURA TARO was born in Yanaka, Tokyo. He joined Nakagiri Masao's magazine *LUNA* in 1937, enrolled in the Department of French Literature of Tokyo Foreign Language School in 1941, and entered the Japanese Navy in 1943. After World War II he graduated from Tokyo University, majoring in French literature and was an active member of the Arechi group, portraying the postwar world in his poetry as a contemporary "Waste Land." He also translated some of the works of Ernest Hemingway and Graham Greene.

Faint Light

Basking in the slanted rays of the setting winter sun,
the dog is asleep
with its front paws stretched out on the stone step,
its aged chin
resting on them.

In the age of cruelty
the heavy silver collar
and the heavy chain glistened bright
at the beginning of my dark life.
A series of images scratched by my claws is all I can remember.
February comes around
    and then March.
(Thrown in the stove,
the coal burns brightly, crackling.
Silently, as usual,
my master browses through a book of history,
occasionally raising his fire-flushed face to the cold wind rustling
    over the roof.)
April comes around
    and then May.
Always lifting my eyes up
I used to run around street corners, tracking the smell of urine.
June comes around
    and then August.
That's right,
I have learned some servile tricks

just to get a piece of meat.
The tap water in autumn is nice and cool.
A glassful of water moistens my fangs, dampening my bestiality.
November comes around
   and then December.

Basking in the setting winter sun, in the flow of endless time –
I wonder if that aged nose is blankly sniffing
the end of life.

Yokohama

SUMMER, 1960

This is a dirty sea, colored just like *café au lait*,
like the mouth of a flooded river. Moreover,
vinyl bags, waste straw, and other dubious objects are floating in it.
Disappointed, I chew a piece of gum. Nevertheless,

the harbor has wonderful lights and sounds. The
many cargo ships look majestic under the green summer sky. Oh,
numerous countries, maps, desires, and laws!
A freshly painted blue ship
and a ship with a rusty hull dotted with barnacles are moored to the same buoy.
Beyond the mooring ropes, between the white and red lighthouses
a gray tanker pulled by a blue tugboat, moves in.

As in a photo taken with the lens fully stopped,
masts of orange and brown stand thick, side-by-side,
and the crane of the dock looms up, replacing the after-image of seagulls.
The noise of rivet guns, the whistles sounding like yawning saxophones,
the tongues of waves lapping the ever-gloomy walls of the berths like cats,
the squeak of the hot rubber wheels of a taxi going full speed
from the main pier toward downtown – in the taxi the cute,
   suntanned girlfriend
of an American serviceman was puffing on a cigarette. But still,

I like the smells of the harbor. The white uniform of the chief officer,
and the sweat of the young overworked longshoreman smelling of grease –

they are all wonderfully romantic.
(As a boy I wanted to be either a plumber or a fireman aboard a cargo ship.)
Feeling satisfied now, I spit out my chewing gum, take my sunglasses
out of my pocket, and put them on. Slowly I begin once again to study
the code flags on the masts and the marks on the smokestacks.

Birds

I like birds. Creatures living
in water are foolish. Creatures crawling
on the ground or moving in the earth are base.
Butterflies, winged ants, or bees, dancing in the grass, are short-lived.

When I hold a bird in my palm, it feels warm.
It has rich feathers and wise eyes, and is intrepid, determined, and lonely. But
many as its virtues may be, its feet are horrifying. They look
exactly like the hands of a dying man in agony.

 – Clouds, piling one on top of another at a low altitude,
begin to move in slowly. A quick, heavy shower comes; then suddenly
a patch of blue sky appears. Toward the center of the light
a bird soars in a straight line. Well,

I am a human being, an animal that stands upright
by means of idea and imagery, a meat grinder
manufacturing hatred and desire. Therefore,
I am especially fond of the bird's living, yet stiffened, feet.

Tamura Ryuichi | (1923–)

TAMURA RYUICHI, born in Otsuka, Tokyo, is one of the most important postwar poets in Japan. A high school classmate of Kitamura Taro, he joined *Shin Ryodo* (*New Territory*) in 1939, and in the same year joined Nakagiri Masao's LE BAL. He enrolled in the Department of Literary Art at Meiji University in 1941, then entered the Navy in 1943, and was sent to several naval stations in Japan until the end of the war. Shortly thereafter, with poet-friends Kitamura, Miyoshi, Ayukawa, Kuroda, and Kihara, he founded the *Arechi* magazine. His widely admired poems are prophetic, affirmative, imperative and tense, full of sudden, surprising images, twists, incremental repetitions, and powerful emotions. His selected poems have been translated and published by Katydid Books, Oakland University, Michigan, under the title *Dead Languages*.

World without Words

1

A world without words is a sphere of noontime.
I am a vertical human.

A world without words is a world of poetry at noon.
I cannot remain as a horizontal human.

2

By means of words, I will discover a world without words,
a sphere of noontime, the poetry of noon.
I am a vertical human.
I cannot remain as a horizontal man.

3

At noon on a June day,
with the sun overhead,
I was amid a big cluster of rocks.
At that time
rocks were dead bodies,
the dead bodies of lava,
of the energy
from a great explosion
of an active volcano.

Why is it, then,
that the various forms are the dead bodies of energy?
Why is it, then,
that the various colors and rhythms are the dead bodies of energy?
A bird,
a Japanese golden eagle, for instance,
observes, but does not criticize
in his slow circling.
Why, then,
does he only observe various forms of energy?
Why, then, wouldn't he criticize various colors and rhythms?
Rocks are dead bodies.
I drink milk
and munch bread like a grenade thrower.

4
Oh,
a white-hot fluid rejects its own fluidity.
The frozen images of flames
are not formed by love and fear –
the various phases of extinct energy.

5
A bird's eyes are wickedness itself.
He observes but does not criticize.
A bird's tongue is wickedness itself.
He swallows but does not criticize.

6
Look at the nutcracker's tongue, how it's sharply slit.
Look at the great spotted woodpecker's tongue, how it's like a pagan god's
    spear.
Look at the woodcock's tongue, how it's like a chisel.
Look at the golden mountain thrush's tongue – a pliant weapon.

He observes but does not criticize.
He swallows but does not criticize.

7
I walked down the road as cold as Pluto –

thirteen kilometers down the road as far as the hut –
along the lava flow,
along the road of death and procreation,
along the road of the biggest ebb tide I had ever seen.
I am a grenade thrower,
or
I am a shipwrecked sailor
or
I am a bird's eye,
I am an owl's tongue.

8
I observe with blind eyes.
I fall with my blind eyes open.
I destroy the bark of trees with my tongue lolled out.
I loll out my tongue, but not to embrace love or justice.
The harpoon-like thorns growing on my tongue are not for healing fears and
    hunger.

9
The road of death and procreation is
the road of small animals and insects.
Swarms of bees fly away, raising battle cries.
A thousand needles, even ten thousand of them, lie in ambush.
A road where there is no criticism, no counter-criticism,
no meaning of meaning,
no criticism of criticism –
a road with no empty construction, nor petty hope –
a road with no use for metaphors, symbols, or imagination.
Only destruction and reproduction are there.
Only re-creation and fragments are there.
Only fragments and the fragments of fragments are there.
Only broken pieces and the broken pieces of broken pieces are there.
Only a ground design of a grand ground design is there.
A road of metaphors in cold June.
Air sacs extending from vermilion lungs.
With the air sacs like ice bags filling air to the marrow,
birds fly,
birds fly among birds

10

A bird's eyes are wickedness itself.
A bird's tongue is wickedness itself.
He destroys but does not build.
He re-creates but does not create.
He is a fragment – a fragment among fragments.
He has an air sac but not an empty heart.
His eyes and tongue are wickedness itself, but he is not wicked.
Burn, birds.
Burn, birds, every one of you.
Burn, birds, small animals, every small animal.
Burn, death and procreation.
Burn, road of death and procreation.
Burn.

11

In June as cold as Pluto,
I run down a road as cold as Pluto,
down the road of death and procreation.
I drift about.
I fly.

I am a grenade thrower
and a brave enemy.
I am a shipwrecked sailor,
but I am also an ebb tide.
I am a bird,
and a hunter with crushed eyes.
I am a hunter.
I am an enemy,
a brave enemy.

12

I will finally reach the hut
at sundown.
The short, skinny shrubbery will turn into great forests.
Even the lava flows, along with the sun and the ebb tide,
will be stopped by my small dream.
I will drink a glass of bitter water.
I will drink it as gently as I would drink poison.

I will close my eyes and open them again.
I will mix whiskey with water.

13
I will not return to the hut.
I cannot dilute words with meaning
as I dilute whiskey with water.

Invisible Tree

I saw little tracks in the snow.
Looking at them,
I saw for the first time
the world that is governed by small animals,
little birds and beasts in the woods.
Take a squirrel, for instance.
Its tracks come down an old elm,
cross the trail,
and disappear into the fir woods.
There is no momentary hesitation, no anxiety, no clever question mark.
Or take a fox, for instance.
His tracks go endlessly in a straight line
down the valley road north of the village.
The hunger I know has never drawn
a straight line like his.
My heart has never had
such a resilient, blind, affirmative rhythm as in these tracks.
Or take a bird, for instance.
Its tracks are clearer than its voice,
the print of its claws sharper than its life.
Its wings are printed on the slope of snow.
The fears I've known have never drawn
such a simple pattern.
My heart has never had
such a sensual, heretical, affirmative rhythm as in these wingprints.

Suddenly the huge setting sun hangs on the summit of Mt. Asama.
Something makes forests,
pushes open the mouth of the valley,

rips apart the cold air.
I return to the hut.
I make a fire in the stove.
I am
an invisible tree,
an invisible bird,
an invisible small animal.
I think only
of the invisible rhythms.

Hoya

The town of Hoya is now
in autumn.
I am now
in misery.
My heart has good reason and deep-rooted cause
for being miserable.

The scorching summer is over at last.
The autumn wind blows from one end of the Musashino Plains to the other.
On this spot in the dark Musashino Plains, the silent Musashino Plains,
sits my small home.
In this small home
is my small room
In this small room
I light a small lamp
and work at being miserable
until the deepening misery in my heart takes root
in the ground and grows as huge
as that *keyaki* tree in my bleak back yard.

Tanigawa Gan | (1923–1995)

TANIGAWA GAN was born in Minamata, Kumamoto Prefecture, and graduated from Tokyo University with a major in sociology. He joined the Boin (Vowels) group and wrote highly imaginative revolutionary poetry. In 1947 he joined the Japan Communist Party. He suffered from tuberculosis and returned to Kumamoto to recuperate. His first book of poems, *Daichi no Shonin* (*A Merchant of the Earth*, 1954), presented his revolutionist philosophy expressed with symbolist technique and filled with unconventional, brilliant metaphors. In 1960 he left the Communist Party and later stopped writing poetry.

Merchant

I will be a merchant of the earth.
I will sell mushrooms, the bitterest tea,
rainbows with one color missing,

grass that grows stiff and itchy toward evening,
lonely manes, the blue of animal hooves,
and cobwebs. And with my profit from all these

I will buy some crazed wheat,
a large used republic.
If all these ventures turn to misfortune,

I will pack up cold time.
I will put light into the measure...

Well, my account book lies in the woods.
Rude numerals are dead under the rocks.

How easily fool's gold all over the world rusts,
even in this bright, broad daylight!

A Mill-Hand's Diary

The various philosophies have long since stopped revolving.
This cottage in the south is wet with bitter dew.

While living in view of trees with bark like fish scales, I will make
a small harp of fingernails and hair.

The shoes I used to draw water from the spring are cracked and broken.
Still, under the deceitful sky – an imposter smeared with mud –
in the town where the blood of the Kumaso clan flows purple,
I once knew power.

Listen. The evils of the secretary-general have been made public
and civilization has gradually gone crazy.

Surrounded by ivies, warts, and thorns,
the politburo on this side of the desert has turned into a cocoon.
Piercing every leader's heart while consoling all our mothers,
socialism has aged beyond recognition.

Silently I finish my meal of moonlight.
I chase an ugly chicken as it scurries through a negative world
toward the modest inn of dawn.

The musty king, who doesn't even own an umbrella,
walks around, peeping into a hot pot at every door,
twitching his nose at his domain, where morning-glories thrive,
trampling on a blue that is . . . rather like that of Okinawa.

Morning in a Foreign Land

You people who are about to depart for the east:
Plant your hatred in the garden of dawn
and stand around, waiting.
Plant it in your sister's breast, and leave.
For the locomotive engineer whose bride has been stolen
the sago palm splays out its reddish cotton this morning
and wipes sunrise over the hometown.

On skin, with thick juice squeezed out of the grass,
write out a line that is not afraid of torture.
On the slightly greenish cornea of the young man who is sprinkling water,

please inscribe for the record
tedious parting words in the Ural-Altaic language.

Toward the mountain where mushrooms are burning
the stationmaster blows his whistle.
Now the photograph of this place of exile, smiling forever,
shines in the morning sun,
and the small garden with brown spots
begins to walk, embraced by smoke,
with the hatred of glass eyes planted in it.

Shono Kokichi | (1924–1991)

SHONO KOKICHI was born in Tokyo. He studied political science and German at Tokyo University, where he became a professor of German literature. Rilke was the subject of his graduation thesis, and he also showed special interest in the poetry of Stefan George, Mallarmé, and Kitahara Hakushu. Shono was a member of the Rekitei group.

As It Goes Down

As it goes down, the evening sun grows pale.
In the sphere of dim light
ice-colored clouds break up, stiff.
Flasks, tears,
a human cheek shining with downy hair.
Only white cedars sway ceaselessly
in the wind's slight breathing.
In the awesome, familiar hollow
we call *sky*,
we press on like anxiety. Everything falls way down
and perishes endlessly in silence.
The axis tilts sharply
at an angle of dark solitude. Oh!
a bird, as if being thrown, flies ... where to?

The Water Dashes

The water dashes, gathering into transparent ridges.
Over the pale surface of the expanse
of spreading water, overflowing into the hollows,
the capricious wind throws light and shadows.
Another gust passes.
Glints on the ripples scintillate everywhere
in its moment of reverberation.

Something touches the human heart.
Something touching rises in the expanse of sky.

The mesh of cirrus clouds
is constantly fogged
by thin, shredded clouds scuttling by.
The sunlight, too, is filtered mournfully.
through transluscent atmosphere, the gale spreads its
    soundings
        far and near.

On the Day of the Typhoon

The wheat is already deep green,
and its luster now seethes, now fades,
in its streaming patterns.
The hills are buffeted by the typhoon.
They all glisten
in the blinding, bright zone of the storm.

The gales turn over the blue bottom of the sea,
exposing it to bright daylight, flipping over everything
that can be turned at all,
whipping the water right out of the puddles.
It's spring. Spring. My powerful spring.
The cool air streams by.
Oh, gales that blow vigorously through the pines and white cedars.

In the center of the swaying expanse of space
I stand firmly, perspiring.
Let a song of infinite movement again touch my solitary heart.
Shine, you old sun, shine on my soul, shrunken with cold,
you buoyancy itself,
a catalyst of joy, a spurt of fire!
Just let the composition of beauty, of the sheer beauty
in everything there is, shine brightly for a moment
in the eyes of this mortal being.

Yoshimoto Takaaki | (1924–)

Yoshimoto Takaaki was born in Tokyo. He graduated from Tokyo Institute of Technology in 1947, with a major in electrochemistry, but after two books of poetry in 1952 and 1953, he enjoyed a reputation as a leading radical poet. Abstract as it is at times, his poetry is full of fresh imagery, pleasing rhythms, high energy, and controlled power. Yoshimoto is also one of the foremost of Japan's literary critics. In 1960, he was among the influential leaders of the anti–U.S.-Japan Security Treaty movement. He is a prolific author with books in literary theory, political philosophy, religion, linguistics, and psychology.

A Song to be Sung in Summer

Far away from us, the sea sings in midsummer.
The cathedral dome and the buildings we can see from the wharf sing.
Our hearts sing with an indescribable loneliness.
Insects and grasses sing in moisture and flame.

Oh, these are the songs passed down to us
from one dark purgatory to another.
These are the songs woven with destiny and rebellion,
to be passed on to the future.
Indeed, we let our love and hatred proceed from sorrow to sorrow,
taking our stance in the predestined plan.
While summer covers us with sunshine and wild fatigue,
it also enshrouds us in powder smoke and star-spangled nights.

We are so foolish
that we cannot separate our hearts from our sensitivity.
We take in so many wrong signals
that we cannot explain them to anyone else.

Whatever we have to hide, the night covers it up.
Yet, sometimes, it carves the walls of tall buildings with its sharp blade
and makes all the horn-like stars glitter brightly.

A Song of Our Self-Admonition

Let us become the wings of June's birds
and somersault through the leaden texture of the sky.
The immovable dark center of the world
is fastened to the seasonal sap and the winds,
awaiting our strange visual sense
in a place where, if we tried, we might see.

We move much too lightly
and we do not use the methods prepared for us.
Let us make the color of the blood of our fate
out of the admonitions from a prophetic few in the world.
Soon, wherever we go,
we will meet night closed down with war-fire and sad imagination.
Rejected by its atmosphere,
let each of us become a stubborn solitary.

Even when the stars brush past our wings
with their sharp-edged light
and the swollen winds replace beautiful dreams with death,
we will throw away some of our humility
and bare our pagan claws.

My Boyhood

When I go down into anecdotes from my boyhood,
as if going into dark underpasses,
what speaks to me
is the unfamiliar woman who owned the candy store
and a memory that is stuck
on a cheap piece of candy.
As young comrades, we stole things,
fell into thinking at the edge of a bridge,
bet on marbles,
and forgot the promises made for the following day.
Our world had its own strange laws and lynching,
and those ostracized were exposed to cold winds.
They soon banded together, chose their chief, protected their interests,

and loved their own kin.
Those ostracized rebelled,
came to terms with love and hate,
and when they began to see
the invisible relationships
that could endure the tragic play of the soul,
they broke away with a deep resolve.

When I am about to say
that only disobedience can set free the memories of one's childhood,
I am expelled according to the law of my childhood itself.

Yamamoto Taro | (1925–1988)

Y AMAMOTO T ARO was born in Omori, Tokyo. He studied German literature at Tokyo University. Toward the end of World War II he was assigned to a special-attack speedboat unit, which made him face sudden death squarely and greatly affected his career. His release from that crucial situation led him to reassess his life and work. He started a poetry magazine, *Reido*, with Naka Taro and Kanai Choku, and he joined the Rekitei group. Freely using both archaic and colloquial language, his poems are grand in scale, reaching back for the origins of human experience. "My Poetry Is Direct," the selection here, displays his personal view of poetry.

My Poetry is Direct

1
I cry, I laugh, I groan, I sing –
that's my poetry
I fear, I stammer, I struggle –
that's my poetry
I do not think
but feel –
and that's my poetry

2
I am not a rope that ties down ideas
nor am I a vat of emotions
I am not thin in contours
nor am I fat in meaning
god, the sun, and love
– these spherical systems –
could not be farther away

3
I am procreation and disintegration
nothing but mere movement, so to speak
I am not the traveler who sleeps fulfilled
at the end of his long meditative walk
I am not dragged along with others

4
my poetry is direct
it is more like time than like life
my poetry has direction
it is more like the wind than time

5
do you know the wind's biography?
the wind eats fantasies
the wind has no home
doors and windows are always built
so it can escape

6
the wind was naturally born of fire
when I close my eyes
I see a streak of flame
but that fire is too remote
do you know the mystery
of that primordial wind
that comes to me
in the form of a streak of fire?

7
The fire of that wind burns my face
from behind
then my poetry
pierces through me
on the way to its target

8
I may be nothing but a cold gun barrel
nothing but a tube
which is consumed
by that which hurtles past
scorching me
every word comes through a hole

9
my poetry however is
no bouquet dedicated to *eternity*
it is a pale steel rod
among the pliant stalks
that sway in life's flowerbed
aimed quietly at you
my poetry is *negation.*

10
uh-oh, I got careless and said "you"
it's a bad habit of mine
it's not good to be so vague about someone's name
I am a hunter but
my shooting is not masturbation for me
it is my profession to kill

11
locating, chasing, and making decisions
a hunter pursues himself
together with his game
four eyes confront each other
and call each other "you"

12
a hunter is not a human being
nor is he a beast
he's a wind
unless one becomes a wind one cannot conquer a beast
unless one becomes a wind that can shake the forest
one cannot embrace a beast

13
my game is not, after all, a quadruped
I said I was a *negator*
what I pursue and negate
are things called "eternity" and "death"

14
my word goes straight to you
my word does not descend like a parachute
floating down through death

15
freezing, my word becomes a tree
and opens a window to death
many deceased persons perch
on the branches of my poetry
and sing like birds
"glos" "gloks"
"stiks" "stik"

16
my poems are not hymns
my poetry is question and answer
my poetry is not music rising beautifully through the air
my poetry is a storm that soon will swirl and rage

17
a gentle song of death
a rugged wind that carries the fire
my prairie where the hunter and his game
frantically mate with each other
o cloud that rises!
o radiant charnel!

18
but wait: that holy celestial nimbus –
that is not my poetry, after all

Dawn

To be alone is, after all, to be empty.
Lying on this concrete floodgate
my lump of flesh exudes its tears deliberately.
Ah, this tender life –
it smells of coal.

a city shines like mica in the distance.
People there, like pieces of wire, stroll about.
White faces there, countless masks, flow by.
Mommy's breasts, Johnny's nose –
aren't they all endearing because they move within bonds?
I can't help feeling sad.
The day will come when their relentless unhappiness
and their foolishness will waken me
and make me sing a song!
I will put up a fight.
Is happiness possible there?
I don't know…
I don't know, but I feel this clearly:
both extremes are buried among them.
Long live unhappiness!
My legs are in better shape than my thoughts.
I walk down the white stairs.
A rooster crows like a hog again.
It is dawn.
I will move back into the system with great strides,
even though my eyes are bloodshot with confusion and sweat.
I am not in bondage.
I am free.
Although I am free,
I have my place.
Back among them
I am no longer
an abstraction.

Kubota Hanya | (1926–)

KUBOTA HANYA was born in north Borneo. He graduated from Waseda University with a major in French literature and became a professor of French at Waseda. His poetry is metaphysical, refined, and highbrow. Recognized for his artistic perfection, he holds a prominent position in contemporary Japanese poetry. Kubota has translated René Char's poetry, Casanova's reminiscences, and Apollinaire's short stories. He has also written books of criticism.

Ballad 1

Wind, the universe in which you breathe and fly upward
is false space of infinite expanse.
The foot of the sky, the dark brow of the ocean, too,
is your dominion, wherever you go.
But how restlessly baffled is your emotion!
Why do you quiver and shudder so?
What is your vain fretting and trembling for –
chased by an eye – an eye which is plotting something?…

Even if everything is beautifully adorned
with the scent of flowers and the juice of fruits,
the nature of wind, once it has begun to blow,
can never be anything but wind.
Wind, what clings to you is a musty smell of grass.
When you burn the sorrow of your wandering in flames,
you suffer from your own gasping,
chased by an eye – an eye that is plotting something…

Wind, are you aware
of the comfortable ease of the trees, the birds,
and the beasts that stay in the woods?
You could have remained asleep
deep in the mountains of your distant native place,
knowing that quietness is a pastoral joy,
but you are flocks of black wings in troubled flight,
chased by an eye – an eye that is plotting something…

Taking even your own shadow drifting on the water and the clouds in
    the sky
for veiled presences of threat,
you go mad, shout, grow bewildered, and run,
chased by an eye – an eye that is plotting something. . . .

A Voice

Is that a voice?
That sound of chiseling –
the sound of a thin, emaciated hand
carving and chiseling a cloud
in the sky?

The form of something is taking shape.
Whose figure is it?
Your face? Or mine…?
A vision which seems familiar,
yet not wholly familiar.

Can you hear that?
Can you really hear
that sound of carving and chiseling –
the hollow sound of fragments of time
dropping down the wall of a cloud?

The Mirror

I walk quietly toward me
like a silent shadow crawling at the bottom of a lake.
A pure vacuum tells coldly
of the distance
between me and the other me that is not me.

Am I a fish that dissolves?
I drown.
Into the expanse of transparent light through seaweed

the two me's have erased each other's identity.
The two of us are without either death or birth.

Only one simple thing
deepens
the distance between us two.
You, lake that loves nothing but the shadows of things;
futile is the fretting of the stone that can't pierce the surface of your
    water.

That starving, thirsty me cannot go anywhere.
Oh me, afraid of the other me that is staring at me.
A matchless silence comes surging like a wave.
I close my eyes.
You remain – in the void of the pearl in an oyster.

Yoshino Hiroshi | (1926–)

YOSHINO HIROSHI was born in Sakata City and graduated from Sakata Commercial High School. Overworked in labor union activities, he was taken ill in 1949. Upon his recovery in 1953, he joined the Kai group. Yoshino's lyric poetry reflects the mystery and sadness of life with quiet, reserved sentiment. His language is simple, but its meaning lies deep in the realm of the human heart. He has also edited highly-regarded poetry anthologies.

For Nanako

Dear little Nanako, sleeping
with your cheeks as red as apples –

since the color of your mother's cheeks
has been passed whole
on to you,
her once-smooth cheeks
are now a little pale,
and sour thoughts have increased, these days,
in your father's mind.

To be abrupt,
dear Nanako,
I will not expect much of you.
I have seen
how one can damage oneself
by trying to live up to
the expectations of others.

What I would like you
to have
is good health
and the heart to love yourself.

You cease
to be yourself
when you stop loving yourself.

when you stop
loving yourself,
you stop loving others
and you lose the world.

When you exist,
others exist,
the world exists.

Sour pain has increased
for your father
and for your mother.

I cannot give you
our pain
now.

What I would like to give you
is the balm of good health
and a heart which loves itself,
which is so hard to win,
so difficult to cultivate.

A Rock

A rock, sending up spray,
stands against the stream.
A fish with a stout tail
swims upstream,
strong and silent,
past the rock.
In fighting the stream
each thing has
its own unique
best possible way.
It is so pleasing
that fish do not pity rocks,
that rocks do not deride the fish.
The stream flows in its own rich way,

as a matter of fact,
washing down whatever yields to it.

An Honest Question Mark

I spoke to a bird and
the bird tilted its head, puzzled.

Since it didn't understand me,
it tilted its head, honestly,
to show that it didn't understand me.
It was
an entirely natural twist of its head,
an unaffected, beautiful question mark.

To those unintelligible messages
which ring in my ears
like rising winds
at odd moments,
I'd like to respond
like a bird that tilts its head honestly.

Kuroda Kio | (1926–1984)

KURODA KIO was born in Yamagata Prefecture. During World War II he did factory work around Tokyo as a young mechanic. In his spare time he read Russian literature, especially the work of Gogol. In 1945, he returned to his hometown in the north. In 1946, while taking part in agrarian labor union activities, he joined the Japan Communist Party. Overwork brought on tuberculosis, but after surgery he recovered his health and in 1954, returned to Tokyo. Active with the Retto and Shin Nihon Bungaku (New Japanese Literature) groups, he was a radical left-wing poet deeply involved in the problems of politics and literature. His special concern was the farmers' problems in rural areas.

Clouds

Most people
like to watch clouds.

I too have liked watching them
since long ago.

Fluffy clouds on a nice day
are pleasant,
like clouds an impressionist musician might sketch
with the leisurely tones of a flute.
More than any others, though, I like
the dark blue, turbulent clouds foreboding a storm.

They look so wild and chaotic,
and yet
they are moving toward somewhere
in a firm, solid body.

When I look at them
I feel like shouting out loud.

They must have tremendous speed.
They must have tremendous sides.
I want to sing of them
at the top of my lungs

with a big bass drum
and a tuba that would howl like a bull.

Fantasy of a Guerilla

For days I have been walking
carrying a rifle on my back.
The road meanders
from one strange village to another,
but over there somewhere is a familiar village.
I am returning there.
I must go back.
If I close my eyes I remember instantly
the shape of the woods,
the short cut through the fields,
the decorations on the roofs,
the method of making pickles,
the family clans,
the farmers whittling away each other's small fields,
petty status, and the unchanging white walls,
hoes without handles, land owned by others,
forefathers who died in the gutter,
mothers who were driven to work.
I return there,
taking a short cut I knew.
With my rifle ready, I jump out of a corner.
Time to work off some primordial grudge,
to revenge myself.
The village is there somewhere.
The road continues from one strange village to another.
I keep on walking, but the landscape
seems unfamiliar, dreamlike.
Nobody passes me by.
I meet with no one.
I go to a house to ask for directions,
but the house is deaf and dumb
with only walls, without doors or windows.
I go to another house,
which has no windows or doors either.

There is not a soul anywhere I can speak to.
The road is about to disappear into the village
which shines brightly in unearthly colors.
"Where am I?"
"Where does this road lead to?"
"Tell me!"
"Answer me!"
Taking my rifle off my shoulder
I approach the cluster of soundless houses,
but the weapon is almost weightless.
Something is very wrong.
In my hand I am holding a stick about three feet long.

Hair

It was near winter
and it was after nightfall.
She was combing her hair,
black
and flowing,
but I could see neither her nor the night.
She is one with the darkness, I thought.
She is combing her hair, I thought.

Kanai Choku | (1926–)

KANAI CHOKU was born in Tokyo. Deeply affected by the loss of his sweetheart in the great Tokyo air raid of March 10, 1945, he saw death, destruction and the futility of war everywhere in war-torn Tokyo. His poetry probed the transience, loneliness, and evanescence of human life. By submitting his poems to the magazine *Shigaku*, he came to know Murano Shiro, who influenced and encouraged him. His poems have been reprinted frequently in high school textbooks in Japan. Kanai belongs to the Rekitei group.

Mud

Over there, too, a camellia tree shows its plump blossoms.
As I look steadily at them, at those tired blossoms,
they cease to be mere blossoms; they become like human bodies,
    lonely, heavy with blood.
Soon, as if strangled, they will fall. Once they have fallen,
we can see they, too, are made of mud, handfuls of mud.
Like unknown soldiers who have fallen all over the earth,
they leave no trace, know no honor, and never return.

By the Riverbank

A man stands by a riverbank.
It happens all the time.
But not many a man tells
where he comes from
or where he is going.

Why is the man standing there
by the riverbank?
To regain
everything that he has lost?
Or to lose himself?
Every time the man feels the weight of his losses
he has been led to stand by the river's edge.
Surely the man has stood there without rest.
Since day after day is a succession of losses,

he says
"To live is to lose."

And ah,
I hear the lapping sound
of the inorganic substance licking the slimy soil,
an unpleasant sound
like someone eating;
yet, maybe due to its heartless repetition,
I listen to it with my heart at ease.

And one time when I looked
into the surface of the water to see my own shadow
I happened to see the body of a dead dog washed ashore
which I mistook for my own image.
Its leg bones stuck out like white sticks.
And it was moving in the water
as if trying to say, "I want to walk."
It was being washed by the wavelets,
and it was drifting down
on the way to becoming bare bones.

In the middle of the river, occasionally,
life in the shape of a fish leaps up,
and I think
all those things that come up here to the edge of the river
are those whose souls have not been lifted to heaven,
only floating up a little, transient here, for the last time,
and that they sink to the bottom of nothingness
while we look away.

Accidentalism

I had never doubted
that my heart was mine.

But I came to realize
that my heart was under the breast
of that waitress

who brought me coffee
in the coffee shop
I happened to enter.

I could not help realizing
as her hand, quite nonchalantly,
often held and pushed up her luxuriant breast
which would bulge out of her hand,

that my heart, though unnoticed by others
felt torturously crushed.
Since that day I've had to haunt that coffee shop, called "The Morgue,"
to recapture my heart, which has been taken away.

Ibaragi Noriko | (1926–)

IBARAGI NORIKO was born in Osaka. She graduated from Teikoku Women's College of Pharmacy in 1946. She first intended to be a playwright, but, after submitting poems to *Shigaku* magazine, turned to writing poetry. In 1953, with Kawasaki Hiroshi, she started the magazine *Kai* (*Oar*) which Tanikawa, Yoshino, Ooka, Nakae, and others later joined. Her lyric poetry expresses the sentiments of everyday life in clear, direct language. The selection "When I Was Prettiest in My Life" is one of her best-known poems.

When I Was Prettiest in My Life

When I was prettiest in my life,
the cities crumbled down,
and the blue sky appeared
in the most unexpected places.

When I was prettiest in my life,
a lot of people around me were killed,
in factories, in the sea, and on nameless islands.
I lost the chance to dress up like a girl should.

When I was prettiest in my life,
no men offered me thoughtful gifts.
They only knew how to salute in the military fashion.
They all went off to the front, leaving their beautiful eyes behind.

When I was prettiest in my life,
my head was empty,
my heart was obstinate,
and only my limbs had the bright color of chestnuts.

When I was prettiest in my life,
my country lost in a war.
"How can it be true?" I asked,
striding, with my sleeves rolled up, through the prideless town.

When I was prettiest in my life,
jazz music streamed from the radio.

Feeling dizzy, as if I'd broken a resolve to quit smoking,
I devoured the sweet music of a foreign land.

When I was prettiest in my life,
I was most unhappy,
I was most absurd,
I was helplessly lonely.

Therefore I decided to live a long time, if I could,
like old Rouault of France,
who painted magnificent pictures in his old age.

The Days That Would Glisten Like Diamonds

During his short lifetime,
   his very short lifetime
   of sixty or seventy years,
how much rice planting will the farmer have done?
how many pies will a baker have baked?
how many lectures will a teacher have given on the same subject?

In order to become citizens of the Earth,
poor children's brains are crammed full of grammar,
arithmetic, the habits of fishes, and so forth.
Occupied with such things as improvement of the breed,
struggles against arrogant power,
attacks against unfair trials,
detestable chores,
dealing with the aftermath of foolish wars,
studying, working, getting married,
and having babies,
our wishing to have time for quiet thought
or wishing to live a different life would be a luxury.

On the day when a person takes leave of this world,
he will look back on his lifetime
only to be astonished at realizing
how few were the days when he was really alive.

Included among those few days,
which could be counted on the fingers of one hand,
may be the day when he exchanged
the first flashing of eyes with his sweetheart.

The days when one was really alive would surely differ from person to person.
The days that would glisten like diamonds might be

  the morning of an execution by firing squad,
  a night at the workshop,
  one noontime in the orchard,
  or football practice at dawn.

An Unfamiliar Town

When I enter an unfamiliar town for the first time,
my heart beats a little faster.
There is a buckwheat noodle store,
a sushi shop;
denim trousers are hung out to dry,
a cloud of dust is rising,
a bicycle has been abandoned,
and the town looks commonplace.
But I can feel my heart beat a little faster.

An unfamiliar mountain rises close at hand.
An unfamiliar river is flowing by.
Some legends lie dormant.
I soon find out
the mole of the town,
the secret of the town,
the cry of the town.

When I enter an unfamiliar town for the first time
I walk like a vagabond
with my hands in my pockets,
even if I came on business.

When the weather is fine
thin, pretty colored balloons float
in the sky over the town.
Although the townsfolk don't notice them,
I, who have come for the first time, see them clearly.
Do you know why? They are
the souls of people who were born and raised in the town
but lost their lives far from their homes.
The balloon which floats away hurriedly
is the soul of a woman who married a man
in some faraway place,
and she came as a soul to visit,
lonesome for her native town.

And so I grow to like
the small, humble towns of Japan,
towns with clear water, little towns,
towns where the yam soup tastes good, obstinate towns,
snowbound towns, towns surrounded by rapeseed flowers,
towns with glaring eyes, towns from which the sea is visible,
towns with cocky menfolk, towns with hardworking women.

Nakamura Minoru | (1927–)

NAKAMURA MINORU was born in Omiya, Saitama Prefecture. He graduated from the Department of Law at Tokyo University. A lawyer by profession, he is also a writer of fresh and refined lyric poetry, mostly in the sonnet form of fourteen lines. His books of poems have won him the Takamura Kotaro Prize and the Yomiuri Literature Prize. Nakamura also writes critical essays.

At Ueno Station

The railroad tracks come to a dead end, and the walkway widens.
The windows of the huge covered concourse are high, the noises loud.
The ugly station building looks like a huge bird resting its wings
on the corner of a hill. The sky above is overcast.

Here so many journeys begin and end.
We stop here and hesitate.
How hollow it is to think of journeys here!
and how enchanting at the same time!

When I listen attentively in the middle of all the noise,
time crumbles, rumbling like an avalanche,
so many journeys floating like mustard seeds.

Ah, we travelers pass across
a little area of this planet's surface.
We just keep moving on our inevitable journey.

To See

I raise my eyes
but instead of a mountain
I see a city
bustling with crowds of people.

When I raise my voice
it sinks into the courtyard among the buildings at dusk.
It is lost

in the complex meshes of order.

When I raise my eyes
I see order expanding and swaying
like a spider's web.

I see the city seething,
with its crowds rushing
into each of the meshes.

Waiting for Dawn

People waited for dawn, standing on the headland plateau.
The ocean looked like mercury. The night was already pale.
The sky above was clear, while gray clouds hung out over the sea.
A stray dog was running around. A cold wind bit at my cheek.

After a long while, crimson spilled through a slit in the thick clouds.
As soon as it appeared, the clouds hung lower.
A light like a halo was reflected on the distant sea surface.

Nobody saw the dawn. Yet the day certainly broke.
The grass had lustrous dew in it.
The ocean was boisterous with its deepening blue.
Seagulls fluttered toward the hills where winds rustled in the pines.

Then the sun was up. People scattered away,
moving down the plateau of the headland, each nursing some grudge
that was neither disappointment nor despair.

Takano Kikuo | (1927–)

TAKANO KIKUO was born on Sado Island and graduated from Utsunomiya Agricultural College. Interested in surrealism, he joined the VOU group in 1950, and the Arechi group in 1953. Takano occupies a significant position in postwar Japanese poetry for his concise, epigrammatic technique in manipulating words. On the surface, his poems are easy to read, but they inquire deeply and persistently into the meaning of things. Some of his poems are set to music. Two of the selections here, "The Top" and "Mirror," are among his best-known and widely admired poems.

In the Distant Sky

In the distant sky
a hawk
slowly draws a circle

then
together with it
within me also
something
slowly draws a circle.

The Top

Whatever grace
and whatever solitude you may have,
you cannot keep standing.
You stand up only
when you keep spinning around yourself
to no purpose.

However, while you spin around yourself without purpose
what vertigo
and what sense of your own life you have overcome!
And even now,
by watching you spin, who is putting up with
his own excessive boredom?

Mirror

What a doleful thing
man has devised!
Standing before it
means standing before oneself.
One who questions in front of it
at once finds himself questioned.
Moreover,
why is it you have to step backward
in order to move farther inside?

The Vines

Reaching sharply upward
to cling to heaven
the vines catch at the void
in vain
and, twisting,
each madly entwines
with another vine.

Tsujii Takashi | (1927–)

Tsujii Takashi (the pen name of Tsutsumi Seiji) was born in Tokyo. In 1955, during his student days in the Department of Economics of Tokyo University, he was an important member of the National Federation of Student Self-Government Associations. Disillusioned with the confusion and failure of the student movement, he found solace in writing to express his wounded spirit and his resistance to grim reality. His poetry features brilliant, surreal imagery. Tsujii is the rare poet who is also a business executive, serving as director of the Seibu Department Stores and head of the Seibu Distribution Group. He also writes novels.

Quarrel

I witnessed a little quarrel,
quieter than a court trial
or a gambling scene.

In the foggy night
the woman's saddened eyes looked foolish
and the comedy was in its way unbearable.

The man was vexed.
Like a bird pecking
suspiciously
at its own withered leg,
he was kindling humble anger
at the fact that a heart had broken the pledge of the sun.

Tired of big dramas
and fed up with riots and disasters,
our hearts are captivated
by a casual quarrel, one
hardly worthy of being written into a novel.
In such a moment
a remaining flower petal
suddenly, silently, falls
into the darkness
in my heart.

Cassowaries

Cassowaries are
evil lights,
bony,
swollen meat,
sailing in the desert.

I thought only a confident character
could make others feel insecure,
but here in the desert
cassowaries themselves are uneasy.

Therefore they eat fire,
and dash along for no reason,
and then rest.

The sand dunes wander.
The sun is red
but it's rotten green in their eyes.

Cassowaries are
evil lights,
and strut, dangling uneasiness along with them.

Looking at them,
I carefully pour myself – the *me* which has been too much to handle –
into the canteen.

The compass has unaccountably become an obelisk
and will not move at all.

Desert

(FROM *The California Legend*)

When the wind blew
the hills moved.
The naked cactus, irritated,
kicked up the sand.

The evening glow colored invisible walls with red.
The derricks of oil wells became skeletons.
Dead buffalos roared
in the running clouds.

When the man stopped fighting,
he could not go home,
Only the prairie schooner's wheels rolled, away off,
and fish swam in the sky.

Gigantic pages were turned over
and the wilderness of California grew green.
The story of the man became a legend,
living in the weary muscles of people,
occasionally pricking their sense of regret.

The setting sun of California still is red.
Heartless music flows along the highway,
and the hearts of people ride on missiles.
The wheels that disappeared in the desert
never came back.

Ohno Shin | (1928–)

OHNO SHIN was born in Korea. He entered the College of Law at Kyoto University, but contracted tuberculosis in 1949, and received medical treatment until 1955. After recovering, he began to write poetry vigorously, joining the Kyoto magazine *Noppo to Chibi* (*A Tall Man and a Midget*) in 1956. He has energetically reviewed little magazines with sharp critical insight. Death is a frequent subject of his own poems. His book *Ie* (*Home*, 1977) won the twenty-eighth H-Shi Prize.

Man to be Blotted Out

Somewhere
there is an elevator going up, clattering –
a lone man pushing the button, tottering by himself.

Somewhere
there is a man slowly walking down a spiral staircase
like a soldier disappearing into a trench.

Somewhere
there is a man breaking an egg with both hands,
as if breaking a skull.

Somewhere
there is a man hanging onto a freight car,
jerking at each joint of his destiny.

Somewhere
there is a man hiding in the deserted subway,
stepping over the track where a belt of light goes dashing by.

Somewhere
a man exposes
his eyes with the pupils open,
eyes as dry as the footprints of a camel –
from a corner of his eyes
a line of winged ants flying off.

Cat

The sun rises in the fog these days.
It glares in a peculiar way.
I push myself against my front paws, stretching,
and in my eyes sticky darkness still remains.
Darkness is persistent.
My previous life was full of willfulness, regrets, and grudges.
On my foot pads
I always feel a flabbiness of flesh.
A skinny old man always appears out of the fog.
That's my master.
When I see this dried-up figure,
I feel like rubbing my neck against him, just hanging around.
The guy is destined to decay slowly and drop dead in front of a Great Being.
Some day I will lightly jump over him.

I have a fatalistic view of my own.
I draw an invisible circle,
making it satisfying over and over with the legs of rats and frogs,
until they stop moving
at the center of the circle.

And then

I lick at that which can't be erased, no matter how much I lick it,
with my eyes as thin as a new moon.

A Holiday

Following the one-two punch of Gushikin,
the man's shoulders move.
His neck, dodging the swishing blows, begins to move,
and his legs protrude from the quilted foot warmer.
At the sound of the gong
he puts his legs back under the quilt cover.
"I haven't spoken all day, have I?"
he says aloud.

On a holiday, he looks at his hands.
No ink stain on his fingerprints or fingernails.
When the sheets of paper jam in the printing machine, he thinks,
I can't keep my long arms idle.
"Uppercut! Uppercut! Uppercut!"
he yells, jumping up.
Malcarno sinks to the canvas:
an educated boxer, age twenty-eight,
who majored in journalism at college.
He can't get up on his feet.

On the holiday, his wife was out.
The man took his daughter out for lunch.
Just like his wife,
he examined the samples in the window display carefully.
At the third eating place
he ordered Chinese noodles. The only difference was
that they had chocolate parfait for dessert.
On the way home, in front of his house,
a white heron landed on the electric power line.
The way it folded its wings
as it clasped the wire
looked beautiful.
On the holiday
the cold felt mild.

NOTE: Gushikin Yoko (1955–) is a former Japanese boxer.

Kijima Hajime | (1928–)

KIJIMA HAJIME was born in Kyoto and graduated from Tokyo University with a major in English. He was editor of the left-wing poetry magazine *Retto* and also joined Gendai Shi, with Hasegawa Ryusei and Kuroda Kio. He writes poems about animals and human affections, but is known mostly for his critical poetry about Japanese social problems. Kijima took part in the Creative Writing Program at the University of Iowa in America and edited *The Poetry of Postwar Japan* (University of Iowa Press, 1975). He later became a professor of English at Hosei University. He has translated works by African-American writers and also has written children's stories.

Cattle

There flows
the enormous conveyor belt.
The driven black masses are lured out,
cornered into the cold granite mouth.
How sticky is the snivel
dripping incessantly from their nostrils!
The gloomiest rumbles, groans, and commotion come
as from the very bottom of a deluge.
Clusters of shiny black horns thrust skyward from time to time
like the knives of angry children,
some tossed up like a mass of driftwood against the shore.
Even their sexual excitement is a desperate protest!
Shoved back and forth, they jump and bend over one another,
bulls, steers, cows, and oxen.
They cannot see or bite off halters.
The rows of their black backs flow
so irritatingly slowly
toward the slaughterhouse.
Like a flooded river
the herds of black cattle flow endlessly
toward the iron fences of the slaughterer.

Beyond That

I have seen   crazed agitations,
the bleakness of someone   putting himself away,
burnt skins,   the living-body test in Hiroshima,
death's way   in the flight of a moth.
But what can I see   beyond that?

I have seen   the fermentation of evils,
the force of taking aim   with heavy responsibility,
pantheistic brains   which tend to synthesize dreams,
self-deceptive speeches by militants   in the disguise of drunkenness.
But   what can I see   beyond that?

I have seen   the negatives of passion,
the unsteady steps   of a thief running away,
an elegant sky   approaching with its tongue out,
a number of whispers   flowing into new buds.
But   what can I see   beyond that?

More Than Anything Else

We want   to play,
climbing trees   forever,
breathing   the blue sky,
rolling   a ball
that bounces   endlessly.

But
somehow
we are   shooed away.

We like   to walk on,
attracted by the eyes   of a dragonfly
that move endlessly,
attracted by   the incessant songs
of the cicadas.

But

somehow
they   disappear.

Ah,
we are   forever bombarded
by the endless flow
of useless words:

"Watch out!"
"It's no good!"
"You fool!"
"Stop that!"

Where such words as these
are absorbed
by the green woods   and disappear,
and where our faraway friends are,
minnows   will surely teach us how to swim
under a sky   where swallows are darting by.

We   just want
to dance a comic dance
with water imps   as much as we please.
It's enough
to be what we are.

We want to munch
new buds   of wild greens
as much as we please.
It's good   just to savor   a sense of surprise.

We want   to sing
of the freedom   of the heart
which can fly
as happily as
the bird that freely   pecks at its food.

But
somehow
we fall   into silence.

Hasegawa Ryusei | (1928–)

HASEGAWA RYUSEI was born in Osaka. When his parents' business went bankrupt while he was a child, his family broke up and he had to be raised by others. He worked for a lumber dealer at the age of thirteen. Self-taught, he read literature and philosophy, with a special taste for Russian literature. He met Ono Tozaburo in 1946 and joined Retto in 1952, becoming an important member of that group. With his critical attitude and powerful rhythms, he added vigor and a sense of immediacy to the Japanese lyric form. His first book, *Pavlov's Cranes*, caused a big sensation and is considered a significant volume in postwar Japanese poetry.

Mushrooms of Summer

On the dry, cave-like road
in the summertime forest,
tens of thousands of ants in procession
one following on the heels of another.
The mouths of those going in one direction are empty
while those coming back
hold green leaves in their jaws.
They crunch the leaves as they carry them
and scatter them on underground seedbeds inherited from their
    ancestors,
said to be as much as 300 cubic meters in size.
In the dark castle of the anthill
a long time has passed.
The crushed and scattered leaves
have all begun to rot.
On them, as lightly as mist, hang
net-racks for miniature white mushrooms
like small white cabbage heads.
They are summer mushrooms
that nobody has ever seen.

From a Tenement House

Her round arms
could strike

sparks.
She has two sons.
They say that her husband was killed
in battle in the mountains of Java.
She shows no trace of gloom in her face.
And yet, she is meticulous and single-minded.
Was it on a road on a winter night
that I first met her, I wonder?
Her ten fingers that put the filaments in half-watt electric bulbs
and, automatically holding the bulbs upright,
fasten the metal bottoms to them
looked white and enchanting
when we passed each other.
We did not speak to one another,
but she must be a beautiful, stubborn person.
I wonder what she does in the evening.
Does she go straight home from the bulb factory?
Would her children be waiting
for her, with their mouths pouting?

Cabbages at Night

On the thick concrete floor
of the deserted vegetable market
empty into the night,
seven or eight piles of winter cabbages
are left.

Emitting a blue glow,
they light up
every corner of the high ceiling
supported by its tall pillars.

Now a wholesaler
with the collar of his jumper turned up
comes swiftly
into the market like a shadow.
Two unseasonable green caterpillars
that have been crawling

over the mountain of cabbages
suddenly stop moving
as if they were dead.

It is dark outside.
The cold wind that will blow until morning
passes
through thin icicles.

Fujitomi Yasuo | (1928–)

FUJITOMI YASUO was born in Tokyo and graduated from Tokyo University of Foreign Studies, majoring in Mongolian. He was influenced by Kitasono Katsue's 1920s modernism. Fujitomi breaks the Japanese language into small segments and then, putting them together anew in taut verse, composes his playfully cryptic poems. He has translated the poems of e.e. cummings into Japanese.

Mystery

The rain did
not wet the park very much.
A man who looked like a rhino did
not sit on the bench there.
The man's rainproof hat was
not going to spread all over the park either.
A woman built like a steamboat was
not sitting by the man either.
The rain was
not falling like illusory straw rope either.
Superfluous stars did not fall on the park,
and the man did not streeeeeeeetch out like a measuring tape
and reach as far as the sea, nor slowly dissolve in the waves.
In short, nothing seems to have happened,
but something did happen
in this rain-wet park.
I will
just leave it alone.

Today

today a comet is to appear
so the dog
the pastor
and the dragonfly too
are waiting with their mouths open

For

for one very quiet
minute

a cloud floats
over the wine

a moon
over me

the dog has its paws folded

Shinkawa Kazue | (1929–)

SHINKAWA KAZUE was born in Yuki City, Ibaraki Prefecture, and graduated from Yuki Girls' High School in 1946. While in high school, she met Saijo Yaso, a poet, translator, lyricist, and scholar of French literature, who greatly influenced Shinkawa's writing and career. Her poetry is accessible in style and familiar in its everyday subject material, yet distinguished for its woman's perspective and sentiment on human love and freedom. With Yoshihara Sachiko, Shinkawa founded and co-edited the women's poetry magazine *La Mer* in 1983. In 1983–84 she chaired the Japan Modern Poets' Society, being the first woman to hold that position.

The Sole

"Let me take a look at your sole
and I'll read your past and future,"
said an old professor at the party.

They say the path one has walked along
is engraved
on one's sole
and that the path one is to take
is also indicated there like a road map.

Ashamed I might be ticklish
I did not take off my shoes –
but that was just an excuse.

The truth is – I wanted to keep it a secret
like an old diary or something....
On my way home now
I mutter to myself, stepping down hard on my soles.

I have not always walked along sunny main streets.
Memories of the days when I stepped into dark alleys
or forbidden gardens now come back,
and these soles of mine secretly bleed.

A Distant Mirror

One wishes to reflect herself
in a lake she has never seen,
for the mirrors at hand show only
a distorted face now,
no matter which one you look in.

One hastily starts on a trip
without taking time to get ready,
for a voice more familiar
than those of parents, brothers, or sisters
is always calling in the distance.

One feels as if she had stood once before
by the shore of this lake.
It may have been, perhaps, before she was born,
when a cloud was a cloud
and a leaf on a tree was a leaf on a tree.

Chess

We often talked about death,
as if talking about sweet candy
or the newest fashions,
or about a cousin just married
or the old man next door who loves to fish,
and then, as if talking about plans for a short weekend trip,
we would chat about death,
quite cheerfully sometimes.

Were we playing with death,
as if fingering a silk handkerchief or something?
Or was death toying with us with his cold fingers,
as if playing a game of chess?
Suddenly
we looked in each other's eyes, silent,
as if frightened.

In the coffee shop
wearisome music was playing all the time,
and the air was hot and stuffy,
but under the table
the tips of our pointed shoes
were cold as ever.

Suwa Yu | (1929–1992)

SUWA YU was born in Tokyo and graduated from the Department of Literary Art in Meiji University. In 1951, he joined the modernist VOU group, led by the surrealist poet Kitasono Katsue. His early poems used fresh, very modern surreal imagery, but his later poems grew more traditional. Suwa was active in introducing the "beat" poets of America to Japan, especially Allen Ginsberg, whose poetry he translated into Japanese. He also wrote a book of critical essays, *The Beat Generation*. His travels in the U.S. late in his career led to poems reflecting his experience in America.

Green Wind

Which way does the weathervane of your mind face,
traveler in the wind?
Which way will you begin to walk,
aphasiac traveler in the wind?

Now I am in front of Southern Pine Station.
In the transparent
perfectly transparent light of autumn,
all that I have in me now
is the weight of an orange in my hand.
The Earth is concentrated in its weight.
The transparent
perfectly transparent light of autumn here in North Carolina
sustains the lustrous sphere.

A train comes, flickering in the shimmering heated air,
slowly tearing the map of my illusion into two streaks.
Between the crossties sunk in the earth
wild onions display their small white flowers.
Their green should have covered the whole of America.
A train without an engineer should have come
to take me away on a trip with no terminal station.

I like white flowers.
White flowers everywhere and white landscape with green leaves wavering
bleach me,

changing me at last into transparent wind or light,
making both me and the map burn in the shimmering heated air.
That is the way my travel should be.

Ah, traveler in the wind,
your fantasy is easily shattered by the roar and heat of the locomotive.
But I keep waving goodbye
to clean, green North Carolina
through the dirty windows of the New York-bound train.
With love, smothered for a while by the weight and scent of the orange,
with love, I keep waving goodbye.

Morning in Missouri

On a morning when a rainbow hangs in the sky of Missouri:
a fresh, dreamlike, morning rock tune
I have just happened to name
The Rock, Rock, Dreamlike Rock Tune.
Under the Missouri sky, placing a dreamlike record jacket under writing paper,
I scribble several lines on the sky.

By the side of a honey locust
I stand on a prairie in America.
It's morning. I am here.

Far in the distance is a forest.
The forest slowly stands up in the fog
like a beast awakening.
Then up into the sky
the fog soars up,
my words soar up.
High is the sky
where a rainbow hangs, a soul-colored rainbow.
The dazzling morning light shines from behind me.
It's morning. I am here.
I must throw away all my fears.
I must say, "I am in love."
On the morning when a rainbow hangs in the sky of Missouri,
words, be pregnant with the wind.

Riding on the rhythm
of the fresh, dreamlike, morning rock tune,
soar up, soar up, words,
up into the Missouri sky.

Landscape

When I left the hotel on the hill, the sun was setting.
Tokyo Tower clumsily spread its legs like a black insect
against the red evening sky.
On the other side, temples and buildings loomed against the setting sun.
Above the strange mixture of Japanese and Western style buildings
hung a big full moon with an ominous color.

The sky leaned over,
the sun fell sharply.
During these few seconds I crossed the iron bridge of Rokugo.
The water was dark
in the silent Tama River.
In the lingering brown color of the sky
I saw the silhouette of the Hakone Mountains.
There were no birds, no wind,
only the Tama River looking dark.

Along the shores of Odawara
the unbroken surface of the winter sea
in the moonlight,
like a gigantic silvery striped cloth,
vastly spreading, surging slowly.
When the sharp moon hung in the middle of the sky,
I walked in the mountains of Izu toward a bamboo forest.

Kawasaki Hiroshi | (1930–)

KAWASAKI HIROSHI was born in Omori, Tokyo, and started writing poetry at sixteen. He has worked at a variety of jobs. He early joined the Boin (Vowels) group of Maruyama Yutaka. Then, with Ibaragi Noriko in 1953, Kawasaki started *Kai*, the magazine of a group joined later by such prominent poets as Tanikawa, Yoshino, Ooka, and Nakae. Kawasaki is also the author of short stories, chidren's stories, and plays for radio and television.

Living

When day breaks
light suddenly overflows,
coloring every opening in the grove of trees.
Pure water gushes irrepressibly between the rocks,
arrows of morning sunlight penetrate
into the clear water, and
I can see with astonishing clarity the small clouds of sand fanned
by the pectoral fins around the trout's belly.
No one admires the clouds,
and no one praises the sun.
Only the delicate bees fly about busily,
colored with the brilliant yellow pollen of *amur adonises*.

In the distance, people can already be seen
tilling the land on a hillside.
A dog, too, romping around them as they work.
Clods of earth are steadily being broken down,
rocks taken away,
green weeds pulled and thrown through the air.
From time to time the man is seen to stop his hoe
and talk to the woman.
The woman too raises her face,
laughing, to say something in reply.
Her white teeth show painfully clear, even from a distance.
From behind the haystack, children come running
and then are gone.
While sweetfish jump out of the surface of the river into the sun,

the cow goes on drinking a song from the river,
quite undisturbed.

Under the sun, these are the only things shining.
There are no letters, nor any words,
so the sheep are no different from the dandelion leaves.

Yes, while walking along the riverbank I see
that the young man with his sleeves rolled up
briskly washing his horse in the cool shade of fresh, thick foliage,
really loves that horse.
And across the way, I see the river flow
and meander along with indescribable joy
and disappear on the far side into the tall grass.

By Some Means or Other

Tree,
isn't there some way or other
I can communicate with you?
You, thriving leaves,
isn't there some means or other by which
I can relate myself to you?

Bird,
can't I
silently enter you
just as
you disappear into a cloud?
And
can't I locate
between two of my muscles
the knack of making my body-weight ride
softly on the wind
without even being aware of it myself?

Evening sun,
please tell me
why children gather on a slope

and watch you.
Why do children move their hands
busily against their small cheeks
as if rubbing your glow into their cheeks,
while raising a whirl of voices
that is neither singing nor chattering?

Tell me how the sun sets,
how the colors of the woods change,
how the dragonfly's wings get transparent,
how the earth grows moist.
Tell me
how the rough grass smells.

Remembrance

Doesn't your body remember
worshiping fire?
And dancing while wearing bones on it?
And wringing the slender neck of a fowl?
And roasting a goat
and eating its meat wrapped softly in a large tender leaf?
Do you remember your woman right next to you
stirring that balmy brown stew
for a long, long time?
Do you remember scratching with a wedge
drawings of a siesta and copulation
on the cave wall in mustard-colored paint?
and that the village chief was older and bigger,
than anyone else,
and had a sure answer to every question?

Iijima Koichi | (1930–)

IIJIMA KOICHI was born in Okayama City and graduated from Tokyo University in 1952, with a major in French literature. He published his first volume of poetry, *Tanin no Sora* (*Strangers' Sky*) in 1953. His second book, *Waga Boin* (*My Vowels*) established him as an exciting new poet. After reading the poetry of Paul Eluard he formed a group with Ooka Makoto and others in 1956, to study surrealism. In 1959, he helped form the poetry group Wani. He published translations and a critical biography of Apollinaire, plus an anthology of surrealist poets in the 1960s, and a critical biography of Hagiwara Sakutaro in 1975. His own poetry is noted for its surreal tendency and its important role in leading Japanese poetry away from postwar darkness. His *Strangers' Sky* has been translated into English and published by Katydid Books, Oakland University, Michigan.

The Way of the Rain

Kilimanjaro on a rainy day.
Kilimanjaro on a rainy day.
Mt. Stromboli on a rainy day.
Mt. Stromboli on a rainy day.
Even the sun is in the rain.
Running lava repels the rain,
causing clouds of steam to rise.
The sun exists at a great distance, far beyond,
showing only its flat shape.

Kilimanjaro.
Kilimanjaro.
Stromboli.
Stromboli on a rainy day.
Cowboys ride in the picture tube by the wall
of a hotel in the city in the rain.
The rain falls on the cowboys, and the raindrops
bead up on their broad-brimmed hats.
The rainwater runs down the men's brows and chins.

In time the rain stops.
The strong sun shines on the horses' backs.
The raindrops on the resolute men

dry up.
A wind stirs overhead.
Or it doesn't.

Kilimanjaro on a rainy day.
Kilimanjaro on a rainy day.
Stromboli.
A torrent of rain pours on the huge slopes of magma.
Tremendous cylinder-shaped steam rises.
Or it doesn't.
Finally steam comes to fill
the room of this hotel.
The sun looks dim in it.
The sun has become only the outline of a disk.
The cold sun.
The existence of a Coca Cola bottle.
The sense of touch develops.

Kilimanjaro.
Kilimanjaro.
Kilimanjaro on a rainy day.
Stars in a national flag, hanging down.
The sun.
The hazy, desert-like prairie.
A woman comes running alone on a rainy day.
Clear lipstick and raindrops are on her lips.
The feeling of her raincoat.
The flesh beneath her raincoat.

Time melts away in the raindrops.
The time of Kilimanjaro.
The time of this place.
Raindrops on the woman's cheeks.
Right here and now
sand melts.
Here and now
a glass bottle melts.
Time is
like sand.
Today

everything looks raw:
breasts and
breath, too.

Imperfect Poetry and Meaningless Poetry

Perfectly tired
of being caught perfectly
in fiction that is perfection,
I try to write imperfect poetry with perfect imperfection;
but I can only write imperfect poetry
imperfectly.

Fed up
with meaningful poetry,
I try to write
meaningless poetry,
but
nothing can be more difficult
than writing meaningless poetry.
Words have meaning –
infinite meaning – and meaning multiplies, multiplies;
words counterblow,
never ceasing to insist
meaninglessly
that they cannot help meaning by any means.

A Spoon

(ON VIEWING THE RELICS OF AUSCHWITZ, JANUARY 1961)

A burnt, rusty spoon makes the sunlight
more blinding,
so blinding that it is hard to see.
The trees are rustling.
This must be a spoon
that someone used to eat with.
What did that person look like? What did he do?

We can easily guess
since he was human like us,
and we can clearly suppose
that he thought the sunlight blindingly bright,
that he loved the rustling trees;
but we don't know the kind of person who killed him
here in Auschwitz.
It is hard for us to picture him
in our imagination.
Only the spoon
taken out of the stained handkerchief
speaks infinitely
and pulls us back relentlessly
to that year which we thought we knew.
The sunlight
of January
spreads silently.
The trees are still rustling. They never stop swaying.

Tada Chimako | (1930–)

TADA CHIMAKO was born in Fukuoka and lives in Kobe. She graduated from Keio University, majoring in English literature. Her first book of poems, *Hanabi* (*Fireworks*), drew favorable attention, and she has published extensively since. Tada is one of the most highly respected poets in Japan. Her style is refined and intellectual, her imagery imaginative and brilliant. A student of the classics, she has shown special interest in Homer's *Odyssey*. Some of her poems are included in English translation in *A Play of Mirrors – Eight Major Poets of Modern Japan*, and translations of her selected poems and prose have been published in *Moonstone Woman*, both by Katydid Books, Oakland University, Michigan. Her poetry has also been translated and published in Sweden. She herself has translated works by Saint-John Perse, Georges Charbonnier, Antonin Artaud, and Marguerite Yourcenar.

Late Summer

In the gentle evening of the summer,
which is tired with the festival,
the water is clear
and the fish are at the bottom.

Holding leftover wreaths
in their languid arms,
trees are
already dreaming.

The last bird has flown by,
holding a black sound
in its beak.

Farewell, summer,
quicken your pace as you go…
Stars fall quietly into the water…

ODYSSEY *or On Absence*

1

You, Odysseus, trainer of the wooden horse of pleasure,
you made your wife swoon in ecstasy with the ardor of your mouth.
When shadowy warriors jumped out
from the broken sides of the wooden horse every night,
Troy burned in the womb of Penelope.

You who started home a long time ago,
wearing around your neck ornaments of the dead gods, killed by fire,
you were always on the waves,
always in the shade of rocks.
Did the seashell dissolve
in the clear acid sea?
And did the bittersweet pearl in the shell dissolve as well?
Is Ithaca still swaying on your brow
like a distant star?
Is the small island still on your tongue,
surrounded by bubbles –
not dissolved in the sour saliva
on your broad, warm tongue?

2

The son grew up, perched on the tallest treetop on the island,
looking out over the open sea.
Every ship could be the special one bearing his absent father,
the god who did not even need to exist in order to rule.

In an extremely angelic moment,
Telemachus soared through the sky,
alighting on the mast of a ship at sea.
Oh, how much like his thoughtful father
the face formed in the crest of a wave!
The mast abruptly tilted
like a scale that has lost its balance.

When Odysseus returns someday
his son will doubt his father's presence for the first time.
He will fall to the ground like a live bird with its wings torn off.

But now
by the flowing current bringing the seasons along,
by all the silver fish living in the sea,
every ship could be the special one bearing his absent father.

3
In the lonely womb – the warm water clock –
your wife crushes one grape at a time
trickling the juice into the empty sky,
thereby gradually relieved of weight.
During the long years of your absence,
the clusters of grapes have all been crushed,
and Penelope is no longer even a woman.

In her hands, worn out in the act of waiting,
the thread will suddenly snap one day,
the spindle that has been turning will stop,
and you will appear out of the shadow of the rocks –
a man who is husband, father, and king,
white hair streaming over your face like the crest of a breaking wave.

The suitors will depart, muttering like an ebb tide.
With wondering eyes, she will look at you, who have returned
to a silence as wide and white as her sandy beach,
at Odysseus, no longer the hero of the tale,
in the sunlight as thick as swarming flies.

4
The slaughter is finished. Let us have music.
The uninvited are all murdered in the middle of the banquet
for the sake of another uninvited guest.

You call the musicians,
stepping over the slain bodies. Let us have music.
(All this while Penelope sleeps.)

The banquet must go on.
Lukewarm blood is poured into the wine jar.
Let the water and sponge cleanse the foul remembrance
while Penelope sleeps.

And oh for some music.
Oh for a flute to comb her hair,
oh for a harp to relax her cheeks
after the ceremony of murder.
Closing her eyes to all this,
Penelope keeps on sleeping,
reluctant to wake from the dream she's been dreaming for twenty years.

Like a Leaf that Falls

Can't a human being die like a leaf that falls
as the season is passing by?

Time forever asks the question,
and space tirelessly unfolds the answer.

And the answer belongs to the stars and the winds,
the forests and beasts and lakes.
Won't nature's design include human beings?

I stand, projecting my face onto the blue sky
like an archaic image of Buddha,
smiling my inborn smile.

Have I ever rebelled?
Is there anything that I haven't lost?
Have I ever been unhappy?

A fish sinks in my eye.
I gradually begin to realize
that I am a happy idiot.

Arms, be the branches of a tree.
Hair, be the leaves of a tree,
I will return to nature's system.

Blow, you autumn wind,
through the space between my ribs.

Sekiguchi Atsushi | (1930–)

SEKIGUCHI ATSUSHI was born in Korea. He graduated from Tokyo University of Foreign Studies, majoring in English and American language and literature. He is a great admirer of Shakespeare's sonnets, the *Rubaiyat* of Omar Khayyám, Dylan Thomas, and D. H. Lawrence. He is known as the translator of Lawrence's poetry into Japanese. Some of his own poems are written in sonnet form. His poetic technique is elaborate and notable for its vivid, vigorous imagery.

A Song of a Magician

My magic is to casually draw a picture
of the sun fit to shine in a different sky
on the title page of your secret book of paintings.
One day, even when you've found it,
I would be embarrassed, all alone
among the numerous stars I shot down,
like a child who has done what he shouldn't.

My magic is to slip a blank card secretly
into a set of playing cards.
While nobody is aware, in the evening,
somewhere in the world, a young gambler like me
should quite unexpectedly come upon the mystery
under the shade of the grouchy joker and heaped-up stakes.

My magic is simple. Throughout my life,
bending my pliant limbs back,
I keep a precarious balance on a net of thin ropes.
Whatever kind of applause I might get,
even if gorgeous wreaths were thrown up to me,
my attention would rather be drawn
to the look of the frozen blue sky.

Song of the Black Panther

I am a black panther.
I am a roguish rebel of the wilderness.

I have forgotten my own mother and five brothers.
I have come this far, wandering out
from the hot cave in the south. When was that?
I have come far, trampling through the jungle in dense fog.
My only comrade asking what this journey is all about
is the sun running around now.

Morning is an unbearable time.
A lone beast, I have no name of my own.
Who says I am so much closer to God because of that?
Now filled only with anger, I raise a loud roar.
Having no duty to perform,
I tear up the lukewarm fog, hurling it into the sky.
With the whip of a curse only I can understand,
I just lash the foolish boundaries of the morning.

I am a black panther.
I am a black dandy of the wilderness.
In my blood I can hear out the sun's beating pulses.
Soon the world is filled with ferocious air.
I polish my fangs and claws against a wet rock
only to tear the smooth sides of gentle animals
and offer their torn red flesh
to the altar under my secret reign.

Lonely creatures and thick ferns of the earth begin
to breathe together in the sweet odors.
I love dusk like this, when prey is plentiful.
Young deer are my greatest joy.
A leap! At that moment, no eye can see
me. Stout limbs cut the world in two
with my black shadow.
Life suspiciously slides up to death, bathed in blood.

I am a black panther.
I am an intrepid fighter of the wilderness.
Not even a star's light brightens the night.
Shaking off advance notice of the miserable rainy season with my supple body,
I will ambush myself,
my eyes glaring in a dark spot of the jungle,

waiting for a new enemy, my transformed self,
an ominous prophet of my demonic world soon to appear.

Ways of Poetry

Since the naked world beckons me, saying, "At least one human should,"
I offer my heart to the world. Dazzled by the light,
I close my eyes one day.

A humble yearning, a slight fever, a fluttering bird,
a voice of the sky. When my heart is filled with plentiful words,
from the womb of the world I give birth to another world.
Stars sigh, and the world stirs a little, at ease.

Though not clearly, I even hear
God calling me by name somewhere.
God sometimes praises me, saying,
"For a human being, you've done well."

Looking back, I see nobody. Uneasily
I prepare myself to come back into the dark world of humanity
with my heart empty, as after a secret affair.

Shibusawa Takasuke | (1930–)

SHIBUSAWA TAKASUKE was born in Nagano Prefecture. After graduation from Tokyo University of Foreign Studies, he went on to Tokyo University for a master's degree in French literature. He later became a professor of French literature at Meiji University. Shibusawa joined the Rekitei group in 1968. His work, influenced by Rimbaud and Baudelaire, reflects his discerning intellect and astute insights.

Song

Would you let me borrow your chopsticks?
The world is always full of mysterious things.
If you could let me borrow your chopsticks,
please let me borrow your sorrow, too.
I will stuff my stomach with a meal of thorns
like a fog at dawn.
Contented, standing on the madness of my dear Milky Way,
I will scatter the stars' pains over the table of nothingness
like thousands of pomegranates.
Let me borrow your chopsticks.

Landscape with a Seashell

A seashell lies half buried in the sand.
It looks at the sea.
Its small ear listens to the sea.
Hugging the landscape in broad daylight,
it casts a glance upward.
Its dry lips kiss the spring.
Sucking up bubbling memories,
half buried in the breathing sand,
the single seashell still hungers.

There is a milestone
for an old man from the mountains,
there is the sail of a ship
for a boy dreaming of a voyage,

and a mother would kneel before the *dagoba* shrine,
grieving for her son who drowned himself.

An air of futility surrounds
the pathetic fragments of Time.
Hills and clouds watch
the seashell which
the waves have secretly dropped.
Even the figures of birds on the white canvas
are not all illusions;
but how helpless the seashell is – unable to turn over even once,
unable to stretch itself even once.

The Blind Lion

Whose voice it is he doesn't know,
but someone's derisive voice
always freezes his heart hard.
He roars with all his might,
"I am king here.
Anyone who sets himself against me will be killed."
But he cannot drown out the derisive voice
of someone – who it is he doesn't know.

In his sense of pride in himself,
this is a primordial jungle,
still bright in the moonlight,
where many kinds of game must be hiding
in the dark, looming forests.
He opens his sightless eyes wide,
and, shaking his body,
he begins to run, roaring, "arrRRR!"
Then his nose is smashed painfully
by a tremendous hard object.
Raging now with hatred,
burning with revengeful intent,
he bleeds miserably.
The lion is furious, but now
he has no trace of his former dignity.

Every time he roars, "I'll kill you all,"
his shabby ribs show like frames of a broken lantern
from under his ostentatious mane.

The iron cage stands isolated
outside time.
He scratches hard at the kingdom of humiliation
with his claws,
and feeling where he is for sure,
still he roars toward the wilderness,
brightened by moonlight
in his sightless mind.

One day, exactly like this,
I roared with a loud voice, aimlessly.
Then the whole world fell upside down
at an angle slanting 130 degrees.
I lived in an upside-down world.
My poetry was a sketch of the anti-universe.
The anti-universe is a terrorist.

Katagiri Yuzuru | (1931–)

KATAGIRI YUZURU was born in Tokyo. He completed Waseda University's master's program in English and studied at San Francisco State University in 1959, as a Fulbright Scholar. His *Beat Poetry*, a collection published in 1962, introduced "beat"poets to a wide readership in Japan. His own book of poetry, *Senmonka wa Hoshuteki da* (*Experts Are Conservative*, 1964) satirized the politics and customs of the 1960s. Katagiri has published poems in English. He is also an expert in linguistics and teaches at Seika University in Kyoto.

Childhood

Ordinary grownups praised my drawing,
but my art teacher was not pleased with it.
"Don't draw every individual tree branch like that.
You must draw according to your overall impression.
And those are cold colors you are using."
So said my art teacher.
Reading his comments
my mother would say,
"That's because your heart is cold,
unkind, and inconsiderate.
Why can't you be more warm-hearted?"

At dinnertime, for instance, if I said,
"We had lots of fun playing sword-fight,"
I knew my mother would say,
"What if a stick got poked in your eye
playing like that? And when you climb that fence,
what if it fell? Besides,
I don't want you to play with that boy."
And if I said something like this,
"Our art teacher is going
to give us special lessons after school,"
she'd be sure to say, "Well, then,
do get the special lessons,"and I wouldn't have time to play,
so I decided not to tell her what happened during the day.

A Poem to be Continued by the Reader

While playing at a construction site,
a two-year-old child slipped, fell into a concrete pipe,
and got stuck halfway in.
The rescue work took too long, and the child was dead,
although no one meant it to turn out that way.

At a curved railroad crossing the motorman noticed a truck
stuck with engine trouble, and he slammed on the brakes.
But a train going forty mph skids 400 yards before coming to a stop,
so the first two cars fell into a riverbed, with five dead and 205 injured.
The motorman was arrested,
although he didn't do it intentionally.

Napalm bombs are made for burning things, intentionally;
pineapple grenades are made for intentional killing;
machine guns and rifles are also made for intentional killing;
but the guys who make them don't get arrested –
just those who hand out bills saying "Stop Making Weapons,"
they get arrested.

A Wind

A wind is passing
between sea and mountain.
A wind is passing by.
It is the Earth breathing.

A wind is passing
between hair and nape.
A wind is passing by,
stroking the grass.

A wind is passing
between skin and clothes.
It's very pleasant
to feel the wind passing through.

A wind is passing
through the space between lips.
A wind is passing by,
turning into song.

A wind is passing
through arms in a scrimmage.
A wind is passing by,
stirring up dust.

A wind is passing
between words and actions.
A wind is passing by,
stirring up songs.

A wind is passing
between the night and morning.
That a wind is passing by
is proof it is alive.

Ooka Makoto | (1931–)

OOKA MAKOTO was born in Mishima City, Shizuoka Prefecture. He graduated from Tokyo University with a major in Japanese literature and an interest in the work of Paul Eluard and surrealism. He was an early member of the Kai group. Ooka is one of Japan's most important and prolific contemporary poets with fifteen volumes of his *Complete Works* currently in print. His creative spirit is fertile, free, and overflowing – his imagery rapturous, expansive, and original. His knowledge of Japanese literature, both classical and modern, and his familiarity with modern French literature are broad and deep. With others, Ooka published *Anthologie de poésie japonaise contemporaine* (Gallimard, 1986). Two volumes of his selected poems have been published in English translation by Katydid Books, Oakland University, Michigan.

To Live

Do we know
that water has many different layers?
Fish at the bottom and algae on the surface
bask in different light.
It makes them varicolored
and gives them shadows.

I pick up pearls from the pavement.
I live … in a forest of imagery,
on musical notes hung on the strings of my heart.
I live … in the holes made by waterdrops on the snow,
in the morning's marshland where liverworts open.
I live … on maps of the past and the future.

I have forgotten what color my eyes were yesterday.
But my fingers know
what my eyes of yesterday saw,
since what the eyes saw was stroked by hands
as smooth as the bark of the beech –
Oh, I live on the sensualities blown by the winds.

Dreams Tap on the Roof Like the Footsteps of Animals

Waterweeds and the sun begin to sway at the bottom of the pond.
Stones awake at the edge of the plain.
Birds that have just awakened
open their nostrils to the sky.

To be alive – why should it be such a mystery?
My morning is wrapped up with the mornings of others.
Ten fingers – these make sure of my world.
And two eyes – these serve as my windows.

Women peel green oranges on the beach.
Insects swarm up and around, chasing the scent.
The women peel the skin of the season round and round.
And there is no mystery there.

The morning light wraps its arms around my neck.
I lose sight of the past.
My open hands hold a brimful ocean,
colored like a map and stippled with the innumerable eggs of fishes.

Like Underground Water

Pushing apart the folds of interlocking flowers,
light spills up from under the ground, and a river overflows.

The road
warms your feet.
The sky
spreads out within you.

Spread out your arms and let them bloom in the wind.
Let us dream of the morning when fruit trees blossom.

A young hand stretches itself in the mud.
I shake hands with the earth.
After years of futility
I stand

under the blaze of a burning forest.

Even sorrow adds to my bones' sharp glitter.
Pain makes my flesh smell sweet from within.
Nothing is without its use.

I open myself
toward the woods where resin seeps,
toward you.

From underneath you, the winds rise,
and your voice hits on the rocks, scattering echoes.
My eyes become hounds and chase all around
over the horizon, over the landscape, between ourselves.

Shiraishi Kazuko | (1931–)

SHIRAISHI KAZUKO was born in Vancouver, Canada. She graduated from the Department of Arts, Waseda University. In her late teens she joined the VOU group, in which she learned modernism and surrealism. She won the twenty-first H-Shi Prize in 1970 for her collection *Seinaru Inja no Kisetsu* (*A Season of Sacred Lust*) and the Mugen Prize for *Isso no Kanu Mirai e Modoru* (*A Canoe Returns to the Future*) in 1978. Her poetry is bold, modern, and erotic. She is one of the most international of Japanese poets and is known to many readers outside Japan as a jazz-inspired poet of sexual liberation. She has traveled all over the world giving poetry readings, which are impressive due to her delicate, yet powerful delivery.

Al's Got into the Saxophone

Al has got himself
into the saxophone
and won't come out.

When night comes, the men
stand on the stage,
but only Al,
clutching the rough sounds in his arms,
hides himself
like a girl, in the dark.

The woman breaks up the chairs
and smashes the beer bottles
and slams the saxophone against the sky.

Then,
held up by the stars,
the saxophone begins to blow Al's hands and feet.

Nick and Muriel

We may be fierce crocodiles
that devour together the short time we have
under the harsh July sun.

Shedding blood in the river,
we cannot forget the memory
of biting off each other's lives
as if it were our first hate,
as if it were our first love.
Oh Sun, any prayer from us who have no god
is like lashing our acts
with our own tails.
And yet, we may be fierce crocodiles
that devour together the short time we have
under the harsh July sun.

Male/Monkey Story

Do you know
what I have been raising for a long time? A female dog.
Crawling all over the bed,
I do my best not to miss a single flea on her.
If I could take a shower of disgrace
for that activity
I would not snivel or whimper,
even though I cannot become a proud mother
carrying honorable love in a pouch like a kangaroo.
Every pouch belongs naturally to motherhood.
I am a long-armed monkey,
carrying my barren maleness with neither motherhood nor pouch ...

Saying, "Shake, shake,
this is the Shake,"
everybody dances the Monkey Dance, shaking his body.
Everybody looks for a monkey after trying philosophy.
Otherwise how could life go on?

That woman loved me too much.
My former sweetheart, she gradually has become a fairy,
noble and poor.
She is just ungovernable,
being a poet besides.
Every night I wait for that woman to drown

in alcohol or the semen of other men
and not come up to the surface.
I just can't stand being loved,
like sacred filth, by a fairy or a witch.

(I will tell you about men.)
As for women, they don't know anything about men.
They only mess up the blackboard completely, powdering it
with the chalk of love.
Every man is (or wishes to be) a naked horse
galloping on the prairie.
Looking to the future at the time,
he has a most rich erection
as he raises his tail, like a broom, alone,
forgetting his barren maleness.
You can't type about those elevated numbers
and record them clearly.
If a rocket were launched
to outer space, packed with maleness,
it would be "Bye-bye, women."
This is an Old Song no longer in fashion.
Women would only repeat their yawning again,
since masculinity has kept its ardent push for elimination
ever since it began to gush out in human consciousness.

So that's why I'm completely at a loss
about what to do with the flea I've caught.
Should I return this lovable, pretty flea
to the female dog in my bed?
While
the universe of her blood is shining freshly
in the whole body of the flea,
all motherhood begins in the sky
like an evening glow.
At the dawn of the womb, temperature and chaos are just agreeable.
The canopy of the vagina is crimson.

I will return
to the bed where I haven't really kept anything.
The bed is white.

Would a tailless woman sleep there
or not?
Yet the bed is always for one person.
I am a long-armed monkey, so
my hands grope in the dark
in all directions, like a blind masseur,
reaching out for something
sweetly and tenaciously. Then I am
also a spider as well,
eating my own head, putting out stuff from my rear end,
groping; I am a spider monkey stretching out.
Right at that point
I hug and squeeze motherhood into fatherhood
and begin to live between the two sexes for the first time.

Yasumizu Toshikazu | (1931–)

Yasumizu Toshikazu was born in Kobe and graduated from Kobe University, majoring in English and American literature. He is a member of the Rekitei group. His first volume of poetry, *Sonzai no tame no Uta* (*Song about Existence*, 1955) was followed by *Ai ni tsuite* (*About Love*, 1956) and many subsequent collections. Yasumizu's poems observe the common realities of life and love and are often set in remote districts of Japan. He also has published a collection of essays about his travels.

The Bird

There goes a bird,
a creature bound to the sky,
an object forced to move,
a rock thrown in
by a malicious hand
from the other side of the world.

The Fish

The fish is still there again today, splashing the mud.
Splash.
It is throwing mud at the sun.
In the nearly dried-up marsh,
in mud that is stickier than hate,
with its one side dried up
and its other half buried in the mud,
the fish, staring
at the sun
with its one dried eye,
is still splashing the mud
again today.

A Story of Verbs

"It will be a long voyage, and it is your destiny
that you plow the vast ocean."
Thus we pushed
our ship into the sea,
kicking away the earth,
and lifted a white sail.
The sunlight penetrated the sail
and the sides of the ship, making a noise.
The sea clung
to our hearts day after day.
Attending to our business,
we sucked in the sea and spat it out,
and sized up the heart of the sea.
To make everything pleasant and to
help bring about a wonderful world at the end,
we lay side by side on the deck
and talked about verbs –
"walk, run, dance, work, sing, love, wish…."
When we had to use the word *die*,
we spoke the word *live*
two, three, four times.

Irizawa Yasuo | (1931–)

IRIZAWA YASUO was born in Matsue City, Shimane Prefecture. He entered Tokyo University in 1951, to major in French literature. Three years later he joined the Asuno Kai group, which included Kokai Eiji. In 1965, he published *Kisetsu ni tsuite no Shiron* (*Opinions about Seasons*), which won the sixteenth H-Shi Prize. A long poem, "Waga Izumo, Waga Chinkon" ("My Native Place, Izumo, My Requiem"), won the twentieth Yomiuri Literature Prize. Irizawa's work is highly elaborate and experimental, including inventive prose poems. Often his poems are not based on actual situations or facts, but create their own unique world with surreal imagery. He has translated and published *The Complete Works of Gérard de Nerval*, and other translations and critical essays.

The Crow

If I fly to the square
and crouch on top of the spire all day,
I am happy, looking down at the declining city,
I am glad, looking at the streets falling apart
under the perfectly blue sky.
And even if pagan blood drifted in soon
and another city were built again,
I would be irrepressibly glad
(ah, for several million years)
crouching on top of the spire all day long.

The Country I Visited

I was crying in a country where everything was brown, for I had lost sight of my brother. Then my brother came back, carrying a big bird on his shoulder and laughing. There were as many as seven moons in the sky. There was a woman flying back and forth between them, like a bee, although she was without wings.... My brother plucked the feathers of the bird and broiled it whole for me. It was night, for the moons were out. It was night sevenfold, for there were seven moons out. My brother haughtily told me to go to bed, but I pretended not to hear him because it was so light, and also because I didn't want to sleep in the country where everything was brown for fear of turning to that color myself. I nibbled on some hardtack which I had taken out of my pocket. "Oh, is that my mother? Yes, that must be my mother," I thought. But I was wrong. A bird had shouted something in the woods. A bird had shouted something. Then the mountain gradually came closer. It had only cypress trees, many of them. But when I looked closer, there were just seven cypress trees, and each of them seemed to be pointing at one of the moons. There was a river in the valley with a wooden bridge over it. There was no railing on the bridge. Rabbits were crouching on it, looking in my direction. There were two of them, to be exact. Something came falling from the sky, and, surprised, I looked at the ground only to see small arrow shapes made of paper. There were so many of them scattered all over, each pointing in a different direction, that they were useless – these arrow shapes, I mean – in giving anyone direction. Again my brother had disappeared. I waited and waited, but he didn't come back. Did he follow the first paper arrow that fell, going in the direction it pointed? When I looked far away, everything looked brown and vague. Gone were the mountain, the bridge, and the cypress trees. In the brown-colored world where there was nothing to be seen, only the moons were left behind. Eight of them now, would you believe it? When did that extra one appear, I wonder. And it was very chilly. That's why – that's why I was crying.

On Love

We walk.
We come closer.
We talk to each other.
We walk and talk to each other.

We talk to each other
about our love, about what lies ahead,
about freedom, about peace,
which are indispensable for our love and our future.
In this burned-out land, a quiet word is most important.
Better than snow falling on the ruins at night,
better than the undulations of sand dunes
is a word that is spoken quietly.

Yet it must be a word as heavy
as a gunstock with numerous deep teethmarks,
burning as hard as the center of a blast furnace,
and reaching as far out
and as everlasting as the sound of the sea.

A word that won't fade
even on the lip that momentarily burns.
A word audible through the darkest, thickest barrier.

We choose it
and melt it in our blood.
We embrace each other.
We are true.
We walk.
We walk
in as many directions as there are people in the world.

We come closer.

Kokai Eiji | (1931–)

KOKAI EIJI was born in Azabu, Tokyo. He graduated from Tokyo University in 1955, with a major in French literature. He taught in secondary schools before becoming a professor of French and poetry at Yokohama National University. He published his first book of poems, *Toge* (*The Mountain Pass*) in 1954, and his second, *Fudo* (*Climate*) in 1956. With *Fudo*, Kokai established his distinctive style, notable for its fantasy and inventiveness with a lyrical, serene, clear tone. He has also published a four-volume set of translations of works by Henri Michaux and two volumes of works by Federico Garcia Lorca, along with several scholarly studies of French poetry and postwar Japanese poetry.

The Bridge

The setting sun hangs over the bridge like a grapefruit.
Through slits in the piling cotton-puff clouds
leak slanting orange-colored streaks of light.

Here in the secluded town,
many thin streaks of smoke rise where suppers are being prepared.
From across the bridge
I can hear the chatter of children riding tricycles:

> "Look. There's a fire in the sky far away, do you see it?"
> "Oh, yeah! Boy, it's really on fire."
> "Look, it's burning such a bright red."

The clatter of the tricycles expands
like a ripple on the water, recedes
into the distance, and fades away.
The sound of a bell tolling in the woods to the southwest
drifts away over the evening glow.
The daylight gradually fades from the bridge.
The boy who went after a ball thrown while there was still daylight
hasn't come back yet.

Genesis

A miasma hung over the island, surrounding it and swaying. The mysterious vapor rising out of the rocks sunk deep in the inlets hung over the island day and night. At night, out of the sunken rocks a whitish phosphorescent light gleamed, like a streak of white flame, frightening fishermen with its weird light. By day, birds flying over it fell, fishes gradually died out in the inlets, and soon a dark, dense fog spread over the desolate sea of death.

One day the island suddenly began to move. In this obscure fog and sea, in the merging of sky and land, in the borderless mass that looked like a dense sea of clouds, the island hung in midair, and nothing went through it except the distant stars, scattered out far away.

Anger and sorrow melted into one mass. And inhabitants of another island tens of millions of light-years away could feel a deep sigh. Shooting stars flew, and then some obscure primordial organism came into being. Destruction called in decomposition; decomposition called in a new morning glow. It was dazzlingly bright.

Everything was to begin there. A voice rose from a spot on the island.

Dark Dirge

A man always comes back,
counting stones of sorrow in his heart
like a wounded king.

A man always comes back,
squandering all the crisp, fragrant air of the morning's glow,
on the day's fixed frame of work.

He carries a silent shadow on his back,
an invisible thread pulling his legs.
Thinking of his great distance from the world,
a man always comes back,
in the slanting lamplight,
to the eternally desolate, still wooden bed,
to the ever-approaching cold fireplace of death.

– It's like a fixed ritual.

Tanikawa Shuntaro | (1931–)

TANIKAWA SHUNTARO was born in Tokyo. His father, Tetsuzo, was a renowned philosopher and president of Hosei University. Tanikawa began to write poetry while he was in high school and later joined the Kai group. One of the most productive, prolific, and popular poets in Japan, he is also active in writing dramas, radio plays, song lyrics, scenarios, picture books, and essays, and in live readings of his own poems. He has a best-selling translation of *Mother Goose Rhymes*. Tanikawa's is a positive, clear voice full of bright perceptions. His first and second books of poetry, *Nijuoku Konen no Kodoku* (*The Loneliness of Two Billion Light Years*) and *Rokujuni no Sonetto* (*Sixty-two Sonnets*), are significant volumes in contemporary Japanese poetry. An English edition of his *Selected Poems* was published by North Point Press in San Francisco, and Katydid Books, Oakland University, Michigan, has published a number of Tanikawa's works in translation.

Mother

The Earth tries to grab the jet plane
and hug it to her breast.

The Earth tries to pull at the submarine
and return it to her womb.

Jealous of other spheres and stars,
the Earth is an obstinate mother.

The Earth perpetually
holds fast to our feet,

though we have arrived at puberty,
though we are old enough to touch the moon.

Toba 1

There is nothing to write about.
My body is exposed to the sun.
My wife is lovely.
My children are healthy.

Shall I tell the truth?
I pretend to be a poet,
But I am not.

I was created and am now left alone here.
Look! The sun falls between the rocks like that,
And the sea looks so much darker.

I have nothing to tell you about
Except the silence of this daytime.
Even if you were shedding your blood in the country,
How unceasingly bright it is!

Anonym IV

On the body of a cat just run over,
the afternoon sun falls.
The soul could linger there for a lifetime,
if so it wished.

But it fleets away in a flash,
leaving so much,
in silence…

We cannot finish talking about anything,
no matter how small it may be.
The content of silence is
nothing but words…

the edge of a cloud shining gold…
the lure
of music…

3,060,000,000 People

Each one of 6,120,000,000 hands is doing
At this very moment
What it wants to do.

A hand rips a flag.
A hand joins another in the dark.
A hand gives a signal for cheating.
A hand loves, a hand kills, a hand is paralyzed.
Far beyond the imagination of any poet,
Those 6,120,000,000 hands are hungry and tremble
Like the tentacles of a sea anemone –
They would never hold one another in a circle.

Iwata Hiroshi | (1932–)

IWATA HIROSHI was born in Hokkaido. His family moved to Tokyo when he was six. Since his high school days he has been interested in astronomy. In 1949 he entered Tokyo University of Foreign Studies, majoring in Russian, but he quit before completing his course work. He joined the poetry groups Kyo and Wani. His first book of poems, *Dokusai* (*Dictatorship*, 1956), was followed by several other volumes of poetry, translations, and short stories. Iwata's translations of V.V. Mayakovsky and Jacques Prévert have been highly praised. His own poetry displays skillful use of alliteration, rhyme, and puns to achieve his artful satirical treatment of social iniquities.

Historical Facts

The carpenter sits
by the fire
near the house he is building
and eats lunch.
The cooper puts
hoops on the tubs
sitting on the earth floor
with all the curtains drawn
till midnight.
The junkman collects rags.
The cremator takes care of the fire at the crematory.
The farmer loses fingernails, handling manure and pulling weeds.
The fish dealer
tucks up his trousers
lets the water run
and dresses fish.
The grocer pulls his cart.
None of them has a place
to sing old ditties
except in the red-light district.
And me?
I will be an old man soon.

Entry in My Diary, Morning of March 27

from midnight on
I smoked
and drank milk
the clock quickly digested
the rest of the night
the terribly vast flood of morning
washes away almost all my work
but what remains at hand
is this my work?
whose work is this?
whose work am I?
who will be my work?
the smug clock looked white and gentle
so I undressed myself
the dream was deliberately tired
and didn't beset me for a while
then the teeth of the dream locked on me
and began to drag me through space horizontally long
everything looks horizontal
rails   flattened rice cakes   socks   transits
women have precise indentations
waking up
I drank tea
I shined my shoes
time to take off for town
I will put the pains of my shoulders and neck
and ribs and the back of my head
into an empty container
and stuff it deep in my breast pocket
that young office worker in that building
I've known him well since my previous life
he spent a million yen finishing his schooling
his father lives alone in the country
since he's hugely lonesome he keeps a huge dog
together with the dog he ought to die tomorrow
go to hell with the dog

Peacetime Industry

Once a merchant said to me,
taking off his glasses,
"I'll buy you! Will you work
at my place? Give me twenty-four hours."
And he marked my thumb with ink.
Well.   Indeed.   And that was that.

Once a merchant said to me,
kicking over his chair,
"Quit writing! Will you eat free meals
at my place. I'll give you twenty-four hours."
And he held a razor against my neck.
Well.   Indeed.   And that was that.

Once a merchant said to me,
taking off his hat,
"Glad to see you! Business is booming
at my place. Twenty-four hours is not enough."
And he rubbed my eyes and nose
as he might a Buddhist saint.
Well.   Indeed.   And that was that.

Shimaoka Shin | (1932–)

Shimaoka Shin was born in Kochi Prefecture. He studied modern French poetry at the graduate school of Meiji University and in 1953 started the poetry magazine *Baku* (*Tapir*) with friends. "What we need today," he has said, "is poetry filled with human love, which we might call 'pan-humanity.'" He seeks an overall restoration of wholesome human life, cursing anything that stands in the way in his scathing but often humorous satires. His poetry is specific, energetic, and sometimes allegorical, with sharp, amusing imagery. A versatile writer, he has published novels and criticism, and has translated two volumes of selected works by Paul Eluard.

Philosophy of a Dog

I'm not cold.
I'm not hungry.
When I'm alone at midnight
I'm really rich and warm.
When you've gulped down your watered-down love
and, worn out with Western-style words,
go to sleep with your satisfied masks,
I crunch the bones of time with my teeth
and slowly howl.
Turning my whole body into a throat,
I unfold the endless, phosphorescent belt of my voice
farther and farther
to the ends of the Earth.
I sniff at the frozen ground.
My sense of smell penetrates to the Earth's core,
to the center of a bright red dream.
You who have looked down on my scenting,
do you think that I will keep on sniffing
at the giblets you hang in the window and yards?
Do you think that I will lick my lips
over miserable leftover food?
I am not pulling at my chain.
My being chained
is a mock means of mooring happiness.
For this you put on a supercilious smile,
but unless you are chained to the black iron ball of the Earth

like a convict,
your ankle securely entwined with the chain,
and unless you are tied to the petty joys
of your home and workplace,
you can't even sleep.
You know
I polish the stars with my tail.
I nip at the night sky.
I associate with a cloud that looks like a bitch with a good coat of fur.
With this hot tongue of mine
I could even lick at the Earth
like a piece of candy.
You are afflicted by your petty dreams.
My ears can hear
the whispers of the universe,
the whispers of ancient ancestors,
the fate of your destruction.
I slowly howl.
And for the sake of my poor master
I secretly connect the broken chain again,
as it was before.

A Guidepost

That which the ant verifies
stopping for a while
in the stuffy air of the grass;

that which a tendril of a pumpkin vine catches
reaching up patiently
in the rain shower;

that which the cicada's cast-off skin clings to,
dreaming of a different life,
quivering in a thunderclap;

that is my guidepost.

It is not one
inscribed on a big stone, such as "Town to the Left,"
directing travelers.
It is a post I drive into myself silently,
confirming my present position after much, much wandering.

Though it points neither right nor left,
all the cells of my soul would nod simultaneously in consent.
Even if I were laughed at as good for nothing,
there is nothing else
that can certify a human life.

Crawling across the dark road
covered with thorns of negation,
I will go straight, sniffing
like a dog
at the distant smell of the sun
hidden on the other side of the Earth.

Blowfish

The moment the hook stuck into my jaw
my anger made me swell.
My murderous intent made spines bristle all over my body.

But all too soon
I was bashed against the hard tip of the world
and my resistance came to an end,
only dribbling salty saliva at the mouth.

My belly, once packed with hot dreams for reform,
was pulled out clean,
and stinking breath was blown into my dried-up skin.

When I came to my senses,
I was a lantern, comically swaying in cold winds
at the doorway of a restaurant.

But I am not quite dead yet.
When that mold of dark desire, my liver, of which I myself did not
    know,
is picked up with chopsticks by those voracious fellows
and slips down their fat throats,

friends,
don't laugh at me, swaying slightly
when lights begin to appear in the drunken streets.
In me
there still is a raging sea.

NOTE: Japanese seafood restaurants often use a lantern made of a
    blowfish skin.

Shindo Ryoko | (1932–)

SHINDO RYOKO was born in Kagoshima City. From age one to nine she lived in what was formerly Manchuria. Her first book of poetry, *Bara Uta* (*Songs of Roses*), was published in 1961. She belongs to the Rekitei group. In 1986 she won the sixteenth Takami Jun Prize for her book, *Bara Fumi* (*Stamping on Roses*). Shindo's poetry is mettlesome, sensual, and full of womanly perceptions.

In a Landscape at Sunset

We see our own aging
in our old friends.
Seasonal flowers, too,
bloom in our eyes,
and fall in our eyes.
The back of an aging person knows nothing.
Defenseless,
it is open to the hatred
and pity of everyone we meet.
Back, you have never been decked with flowers,
have never exchanged any greetings,
and you don't even embrace love
in the end.
With weight from the inside
you get bowed down.
The more affected the heart is,
the stiffer and more formal the back.
It doesn't think about death, but feels only pain.
Our backs have not grasped or seen anything,
but, as if they'd been struck for some unreasonable punishment,
my old friend,
your back and my back are aslant
in the landscape at sunset.
Backbone, you make a clicking sound and revive!
Oh, my dear friend,
my dear back!

At the End of Wilderness

Man,
don't look at me breathing my last.
Whatever it was that I coveted and hungered for,
don't look at me with a judge's eye
while I am trembling with frailty.
If you can assure me of rich daily life from now on
in exchange for my breasts,
please, you superb merchandiser,
shake these jugs of blood and hold them up.

Chorus

Women are beasts always entombed
in the waves of time.
They hide glass beads and pins
in the thickets of fresh green trees.
And they say love.
Men are entirely different beasts.
Crawling around there, counting one affair
after another, they are robbers
and quick-footed soldiers,
running away, without knowing their native shores.
When they inlay the disposal of their game
in their pastoral setting,
men are poets, perfectly.
They are afraid of women deranging the needles of the clock.
Fidgety, serious, and innocent,
they are faint-hearted, tender-fleshed beasts.
They enjoy embracing before they get hurt.
Indulging in it a little too much, they start small wars.
Carelessly, they start big wars.
They lose wishful hopes, poor, vain hopes
over and over again.
Women in the waves of time
never forget how to entwine themselves,
singing arias time after time.
So, history is popular in college,

and calling everything a failure, clicking their tongues,
they talk about democracy or about women themselves,
and go out into town.
Moving out of a small cage into a larger one,
they are foolish beasts.
Caressed after the fashion of the hunting age,
they vaguely think
this is still the way things are
and become a recurring tide
trying to tether their men to be their heroes.
They become a tide
washing the belly of Caesar's horse, swallowing up many a soldier.
The man, trying to restore his vigor,
breathes with more difficulty,
no longer able to respond with what love really is.

The bed is
the beasts' riverbed
passed on down since ancient times.
Water
washes the sun's prow,
flowing round and round the corridor of the womb,
carrying away living things.

Yoshihara Sachiko | (1932–)

YOSHIHARA SACHIKO was born in Tokyo and graduated from Tokyo University, majoring in French literature. Her first book of poems *Yonen Rento* (*The Infant's Litany*, 1964) won the fourth Murou Saisei Prize, and she won the fourth Takami Jun Prize for her poetry in 1974. Her poems deal typically with the trials of love, betrayal, and suffering seen from a woman's point of view. With Shinkawa Kazue she founded and co-edited the women's poetry magazine *La Mer*. Yoshihara is also active in theater, has directed plays, and writes essays and children's stories.

Low Tide

If the gravity of the moon
can pull such a huge ocean as this
a person must weigh a little bit less
on a moonlit night.

The big red ball on the horizon
a while ago was not the moon;
it was the setting sun.
The real moon, with its pale, smaller face,
is hiding somewhere in the back
and we cannot see it now.
The phosphorescent organisms gleaming like stars
in the shadow of the rocks here
are certainly not reflections of the moon.

Nevertheless I feel myself slowing ebbing
from the tips of my feet,
pulled by the invisible moon,
drawing my heart into the starlit water
in the darkening night,

as if I were devoid of internal organs,
as if I were devoid of flesh and blood.

Air Raid

When people were being killed
how could the sky have been so beautiful?

I had never seen such a gorgeous sunset.
Even the clouds were going up in flames.

When I crawled out of the shelter
a fragment of the night sky hissed obliquely by my ears.
Overwhelming light flared in eight glass windows,
one color fighting against another,
all reflected sumptuously as on a screen –

the red struggling to redeem
the blue of day from the black sky,
purple looming, green dashing, orange flowing,
colors of all kinds mixing, shrieking –

was it the southern part of the city
that was bathing in golden rain
falling brightly, god knows from where?
Was it an alien world enclosed within the glass?
Was it silent, dark, heated air
that whirled about, encircling
the dumbfounded little Nero?

How could a war have been
so beautiful?

Of Bread

Don't get me wrong.
It's not because I have bread
that I talk of roses
instead of bread.
It's because I am indiscreet
and have a morbid impulse to eat roses,

and because I have more roses
than bread.

When I am starved
I eat bread.
On the day before I am starved
I eat roses.
I take longer eating bread
than anyone else.

Don't blame me, please, for having bread.
Blame me instead, if you must, for eating roses.

Kora Rumiko | (1932–)

KORA RUMIKO was born in Tokyo. She attended Tokyo College of Fine Arts and Keio University. Her first book of poems, *Seito to Tori* (*Student and Bird*, 1958), was highly praised for its feminine sensibility and style. Her second book, *Basho* (*Place*, 1962), won the thirteenth H-Shi Prize. Besides poetry, Kora has published books of criticism, novels, and anthologies of Asian-African poetry in Japanese translation.

Winter

The water of the river is flowing,
flowing under the iron bridge.

A dark bush is crouching,
crouching under a heavy sky.

A parasite plant is shivering in the wind,
shivering on the top of a dead tree.

Two men are playing billiards,
playing billiards silently.

Three men are drinking,
drinking, making noises with their glasses.

A red fish is swimming,
swimming in the water tank.

The water of the river is flowing,
flowing under the iron bridge.

A woman sits, thinking,
thinking of the man with whom she has just parted.

She

Like the dizziness of the earth
the white azalea blossoms open.

In a jumble of fragrance
the woman disappears.

Flower petals spread at her feet
together with what once was a vision,
becoming a sea of dark vomit,
making her float on it.

Drifting on the endless waves,
she gradually comes to forget
her home town,
the language of flowers,
the sea,
and the wandering.

...between the flower petals of sheets
she awakens
by the side of a man coming to himself,
without life history,
without shame.

A Sound of the Sea

When I feel my two breasts filling up
silently,
I hear a small sound of the sea
in the distance.

The sea flows from the other side
of the Earth, pulled by the moon,
and the ever-rolling waves wash against
my sandy beach.

Thus I keep waiting,
waiting forever,
for my husband and children to come running
and play on the dream shore of my world.

Kawamura Yoichi | (1932–)

KAWAMURA YOICHI was born in Morioka City, Iwate Prefecture, the son of
Christian parents. An early interest in drama led him to theatrical activity with ju-
venile dramas there. His poetry, strongly influenced by postwar modernism, be-
gan to be published in the 1950s, first in newspapers and magazines, then, since
1957, in his frequent books of poems. He was a member of the magazine *Sakka*
(*Writer*) from 1956 to 1991, and in 1985, he founded *Seien* (*Blue Flame*), a quarterly
journal publishing Japanese and foreign poetry. Kawamura has been essential in
the formation and programs of the Japan Modern Poetry Museum in his native
northern prefecture. With Shiraishi Kazuko he held an "Allen Ginsberg in Tokyo"
program in 1988, and he featured Shiraishi herself in an "Evening of Poetry and
Music" at the JMPM in 1990. Kawamura has traveled widely in Southeast Asia,
Canada, and the United States.

On the Sand Dune

Holding a keepsake of the wind in its hand,
a figure stands in silence.
Is it my shadow, wearing black algae?

When I shout, it's spring; when I pray, it's summer;
when I look back, it's autumn.
Is that winter holding white hair in its hands?

The sound of gunfire passes over the dark sand dune.
Who is it, scattering breaths of death
over the estuary of flames?

A legend concerning me has it
that I roamed through palm tree woods with raw *sake* in my hands,
turning my back on the sound of gunfire and the voices of women.

We no longer have love songs of the *Manyo*.
A heavy rain wets down the times of antiquity.
Everything is blown away by the wind through the riverbed.

Therefore, wind,
run through me at top speed, piercing me
under the broken, majestic chandelier.

NOTE: The *Manyo* is the eighth century Japanese anthology.

Midnight Dance

I drink flames

Peeling my heart,
I drink flames under the flame trees in the moonlit night.
On the beach
a dolphin blows a blue rainbow
over the sea of glass with its breath.

Wearing a robe of flame
and chased by flames
over the cracking ice,
a woman is continually laying
countless eggs.

A necklace,
love,
or the seashell's fear.
Tearing up the mourning clothes,
a man keeps running on the sand dune.

Over the lake of amniotic fluid at the end of the universe
shadows of the flames flicker
while unborn babies are dancing,
stirred up and fanned by the flames.

The dance has just begun.

The Sound of the Wind

In the canyons of the buildings of noontime
a shooting star darts.
Chasing after the shooting star,
a girl runs.

Surely a shooting star must come
from the other side of the horizon.
On the farther side,
my dream, fallen through my palms,
may be drifting as an ice floe.
In the deserted canyon of the buildings of noontime,
a rainy season is setting in.
Pulling up the collar of my raincoat,
I stand,
gazing on the traces of countless meteors.

To this canyon summer will come, and then
autumn and winter will come around too.
Oh, the rain and the stars keep falling silently.
Oh, the girl's whisper is fading away.
In the canyon of buildings enveloped by darkness
the only noise is
the sound of the wind.

Nakae Toshio | (1933–)

NAKAE TOSHIO was born in Fukuoka City and graduated from Kansai University, majoring in Japanese literature. He has lived in many places, including some time in Taipei, Taiwan. He is associated with both the Arechi and the Kai groups. His book of poems *Uo no naka no Jikan* (*Time within the Fish*) established him as a significant poet of the 1950s for his keen observations and exploratory manipulation of language. In his book *Goi shu* (*Vocabulary*, 1972), Nakae explored even further the linguistic possibilities of Japanese. To him, vocabulary is itself a poetic motif rather than a means of conveying meaning.

Owls

When night falls, forms of strange creatures gather in the town, arriving from god knows where. They complain endlessly about this or that deformity. Their pitiful beaks and eyes would not reveal their names to any other creature. They are not worthy of the light of day. They become owls full of distrust.

They sing of the perpetual fraud of the everlasting night.

As time passes by, swinging a rope and turning round and round along the street, remaining bones gently sway, and pieces of paper and dusty meat stick to them. The bodies roll like the winds.

The birds steadily grow fatter and fly about and romp from back streets to those farther back, and they walk along the silent streets, muttering, "Oh hatred! Oh anguish! Oh weariness! Oh days!"

Throwing curses at people, they come with sleepless hearts to peck at the dreams of happiness.

A Song of Love

I want to eat this woman.
I want to eat her whole,
without any sugar,
without cooking her.
I want to eat her raw and alive.

I want to cut off the head of this woman.
I want to tear off her limbs.
I want to take off her breasts.

I want to pull off her hair.
I want to keep her all to myself.

I want to eat her song.
I want to eat the wheat fields.
I want to eat the trees.
I want to eat the rapeseed flowers.
I want to eat the spring.

I want to kill her man.
The fish swimming in her, the crawling worms, the slithering snakes,
    the poky rhinoceros –
by driving all these out of her,
I want to let her live.
I want to invite the sun into the woman.

I want to suck up this woman's spirit.
I want to take hold of the clouds.
I want to capture the sky.
I want to seize the moon.
I want to grab the stars.

I want to be with this woman.
I want to protect her.
I want to eat her father, mother, and brothers.
I want to eat even the god which I cannot hope to consume
no matter how much I eat.

The Moon

It is a face –
a face that has slid down
from the soil
in the deathliness of the cemetery.

It is an eye –
the eye of a eunuch
who watches strictly over
the rat-men shut up in the small cage of time.

It is a window –
the window of a celestial factory
with a particle accelerator
that smashes neutrons.

It is a balance sheet –
a balance sheet no ordinary man can read
to understand what it has to say
until the moment of his death.

It is a good white toilet –
a good toilet
that sinks heavily, soaked,
when a small boy wets his bed in a dream.

It is an aged womb –
of one who cannot give birth to truth,
who cannot raise truth,
or who cannot be the wife of anyone.

It is betrayal –
a betrayal against investors,
a shabby figure of the life-manufacturing company
gone bankrupt with too many desires.

At best it is a dead fish –
a dead fish lying on its back,
obsessed, together with the Milky Way,
by soundless music.

It is a chalice –
a big, empty chalice
that man-made men use
for drinking the air, laughing loudly, "Hee-Hee."

It is a rear end –
a rear end lighting up the sky,
a rump of rocks,
of gentle nothingness, of the age of gods.

It is a dream –
a dream of blood
that rises steadily up the still-coughing throat
of a dead man.

It is a song –
a song that reveals
there is no song,
a song of a dead god.

It is the kingdom of death –
our city,
a city where we get by and live,
a city with no human inhabitants.

Kataoka Fumio | (1933–)

Kataoka Fumio was born in Kochi Prefecture and graduated from Meiji University. He belongs to the Baku and Chikyu groups. He has a close relationship with Shimaoka Shin, since they are from the same district of Japan. Together they advocate in their magazine, *Baku*, what they call "neo-fantasism." Kataoka reviews for the monthly poetry magazine *Shi to Shiso* (*Poetry and Thought*). Although he is known mostly for his distinctive serious poetry, he has written some delightful humorous poems in his Kochi dialect.

Chagall

Together, the man and woman,
knowing that my eyes couldn't hear,
talk endlessly with their lips closed,
both hands on their laps in the old-fashioned way.

The door of the house has remained open
for a hundred years.
Someone went into it and soon came out,
but it has not changed at all.

A blue bird stops in the purple sky,
looking back at the treetop still warm.
The moon is wrapped by the sun,
listening to the young man playing the guitar.

Around that time
man and woman in the field are no longer visible.

But
in front of the house with its door open,
a small horse would not raise its head
out of the manger.

Night

Night seems to be a soft plain-wood canoe.
We have not seen each other's face,
and yet each of us is riding in our own canoe.
From now on we need to leave our drifting to the will of the stream.
My wife and daughter, my father and mother –
each of them steals away from me,
drifting toward a distant nebula.
The parting of human lives is not cruel.
As nonchalantly as the nettle tree
casting the shadows of its branches on the water by day,
swaying all day long,
our partings are gathered together
in the painfully swirling nebula of human blood.

I lie in a seamless canoe.
it seems just and peaceful.
I have drifted considerably
and seem to have reached the head of the stream.
In the village of cells that keeps me sleepless
the air is clear.
I wish to drift out
into a still more limitless expanse.

The Story of My Hands

My hands have been full of my ancestors – alive. Since when?
When did I learn this?
Like the lights on the altar
they burn in my sleep.
My ancestors did not plan to breed me.
I bred them instead.

Like the lines in my palms, you were born old.
I don't recollect offering my blood to you.
In the form of my servile fingers
you suck at my life.
When I am about to plough a new world,

you always say,
"No, that isn't the way. It wasn't like that,"
and make my blood coagulate.
Fatigue comes out of my fights with you.

Like closing a book, I close my fists.
I was not born out of your hands.
Nor was I born out of the thin voice
made by your hands.

Each day passes like a sob.
Morning comes.
Where shall I go?
Where shall I go and what shall I do?

The picture-card showman comes daily with his straw hat on.
In his display you still make
delightful mistakes.
The wisdom in your groping
is your clandestine, illegitimate child.

You embraced. You fought.
You even beat each other to death.
Your mouths never vented words of weakness,
but now I feel a faintly murderous urge in my palms.

When run down,
you always went into old tales to hide.
You think you have remained dead in hiding.
I am not an old tale.
My hands are not your hiding place.

You never planned
to breed me,
but I had to breed you, unfaithful folk,
and balance all accounts by breeding you.

My hands are full of good-for-nothing ancestors, alive.

Kasuya Eiichi | (1934–)

KASUYA EIICHI was born in Ibaraki Prefecture and graduated from Waseda University, majoring in commerce. He belongs to the Rekitei, Oni, and Chikyu groups. His book of imaginative prose poetry, *Sekai no Kozo* (*The Structure of the World*), won the second Takami Jun Prize. In 1989, after more than ten years' silence, he published *Akuryo* (*The Evil Spirit*), which won the twenty-seventh Rekitei Prize. One of the most unusual poets in contemporary Japan, he writes poetically cadenced prose narratives that are vivid and fantastic, yet sharply realized and altogether original.

Daffodils

Nobody knows about it but me. I know this out-of-the-way place where many daffodils bloom. Daffodils are always blooming there in profusion, and yet it is an almost dreadful place.

We may call it a swamp – dark, cold, and totally deserted. But the flowers make the darkness of night infinitely colorful. When a breeze blows, a beauty like a cry flutters through them.

Only a white moon and a cliff can be seen dimly, like a false presentiment.

Or perhaps I might have stood there before I was born. My body was helpless, but I remember seeing the same thing several times somewhere. In a fever like a sickness, I think, it was reflected in the windows of all the cities I knew and in the faces of all the people I knew.

Every leaf points at the heavens. When I close my eyes, every daffodil is larger than me. When I am there I feel the fact that death and pleasure combined make a moon, that anxiety and joy combined are a rope.

I secretly tell about the glistening, dew-like place only to my wife. Holding her while she is asleep, I go to that place. There both my wife and I became daffodils just as we are, and can belong to the nameless night forever.

Record of a Strange Tale 1

When we make a wish for the death of a person we hate, it has been customary for us since olden times to take a handful of our own hair to the small shrine at the edge of the village and pray.

Such a wish should be made only once in a lifetime. Anyone can go there in the dead of night, crossing a bridge which is like fire.

Although it is called a shrine, there is nothing significant in it, really. Only an enormous amount of hair is left there secretly among the rugged trees.

Locks of hair are tied to the trunks and branches and are even hung high up in the treetops.

They are old and yet new, remarkably calm and silent.

It is infinitely sobering to add a lock of one's own hair to the countless lifelike things.

As I look back, the starlit sky over our village, whose people make a living by weaving bamboo baskets, looks as beautiful as a rope for hanging.

Record of a Strange Tale 4

Let's just call it an egg. It was something like an egg laid by a young woman.

It was soft and white, and its life was said to have weighed about the same as a Chinese watermelon.

She laid it all by herself on a dirty mattress in a dark house with all its doors closed.

At dawn, after long pains, while wringing out the bloody sheets, all she saw was something like a golden sash hanging way down from heaven, it was said.

Where did the woman go then?

And out of the egg, which was put in a box and carried away, what hatched? No one knows. No book tells about it. Even if it did, it would all be false.

It was a story that took place in the brutal age when human beings lived only for money. Nothing was honest in that age.

Miki Taku | (1935–)

Miki Taku was born in Tokyo. At the age of two he moved with his family to Manchuria. When his father died of typhus fever in 1946, he returned to Shizuoka City, his parents' hometown. Much of his poetry is based on the harrowing wartime experiences of his childhood in Manchuria. In his high school days he read and was influenced by Carl Sandburg's *Chicago Poems*. He graduated from Waseda University, majoring in Russian literature, and joined the Han and Gendai Shi groups. Miki's poetry deals with the conflict between the sanity and weaknesses of humankind. He is the author of literary essays, fiction, and children's stories, as well as poetry.

An Ear

As I browse through the paper's foreign news
in a corner of my room at night,
I can clearly hear enormous human miseries crying out loud
as they fight each other, hand to hand,
on the other side of the ocean.
As I hold my breath, still as a dried herring,
and go over the pages, all kinds of cries
rush in confusion, like the noise when dialing a shortwave radio.
Just as their souls cannot live in harmony with the age,
so our sensitive ears cannot sleep all night long.
In the darkness, our ears hear
the mutterings of many desires.
Disturbed dreams, which can never come to maturity, die away.
You old but once-young men now in business,
who once killed off one beast after another within your hearts,
just like strangling a baby's throat,
you once-young women, who sleep as on a carpet of flowers
in your ephemeral ease,
I would like to stand in the square where you once shed your blood
and become a gentle, terrible ear
that can take in all the cries of the world,
thinking of the one thick rope
that hangs straight from the world of nightmare into the future.

A Family Tree

On the night I came into the world
Mother was madly happy.
Father, thrown into confusion, rushed to the pawnshop
and banged on the wine-dealer's door, waking him up.
Once he had finished drinking the rice wine,
Father worked like hell,
giving it all he had.
By working himself to death, he actually died.
After his death
Mother, in turn, worked as hard
as a hardworking widow could.
By working hard, she sent me to college in Tokyo,
helping me get through my schooling successfully.
Mother, who was born in the unlucky Year of the Horse,
is now sixty.
The once-pretty girl who captivated Father's heart
is now very fat and in high spirits. And as it happens,
a daughter was born to me a while ago.
My wife was madly happy,
and I was thrown into confusion and rushed to the pawnshop
and banged on the wine-dealer's door, waking him up.

NOTE: The "unlucky" Year of the Horse comes around every sixty years, and is
supposed to be a year when many fires break out. Women born in this
year are said to be temperamental and make their husbands die young.

In the Evening Sun

In the evening sun
a town is gently crumbling down.
I read the record of soldiers killed in the war.
Basking in the golden sun,
children run into the light.
Surely that day was like this one.
While I, as a small boy, stood still, astonished
in the evening sun,
the soldiers silently embarked in the convoy.

After much killing, they too were killed.
A housewife, dejected upon receiving the notice
of her husband's death,
wept in front of the family's Buddhist altar,
while the infant played with slices of dried sweet potatoes
on the verandah.
That child was one of my friends.
So we are the children they sired
before going to war.
And we are the children they sired
after coming back from the killing.
When they washed their hands, the water in the basin got red,
and they danced to the tune of "My Blue Heaven,"
and drank the *Kenbishi* brand of rice wine, making horrible faces.
Those who survived like this were cursed,
and they raised their children, teaching them justice.
Oh, in this century
grandpas and great-grandpas worked together
and taught their children justice, while killing people.
We were born of them,
and were raised drinking the milk bought with their money.
So we cannot see what the world really should be like,
and we don't know how to correct it,
because we, already, are in the flames of killing,
because we have abused others and have been abused ourselves,
and because we live far away from God's mercy, in the cruel light,
each of us exposing himself as some kind of beast.
And so, being blind,
we measure the bellies of pregnant women with a dark tapeline
and think of the coming generation with warm hearts.
We shoot at the world with grudges and prejudices
in the town that is gently crumbling down
in the evening sun.

Suzuki Shiroyasu | (1935–)

SUZUKI SHIROYASU was born in Koto-ku, Tokyo. He graduated from Waseda University with a major in French literature. While a student at Waseda, he started the poetry magazine *Ao Wani* (*Blue Crocodiles*) with Takano Tamio. From 1964 to 1969, he was a member of the Kyoku group. His poetry is stark, colloquial, and outspoken, caricaturing latent human desires through provocative imagery.

Luster on the Walls

Inside the stone windows, the floor was stone.
The table on the stone floor was stone.
The bed on the stone floor was stone.
The pillow was stone.
The tableware was stone.
There was no knob on the door.
There was no burial ground.
All the stone was black and lustrous.
The woman did not go out of the stone house.
The man was waiting for another man.
The men indulged themselves in pleasure, holding each other.
The woman was embraced only until she gave birth to a child.
The child the woman held in her arms was hungry and cried all the
    time.
Crying thus all the while, children grew to be men and women.
They never ceased to be, for several thousand years, there
    in the black stone.

A Room Without Walls

Looking from there, I saw a yellow cliff far away
and the sea and white waves.
As I was human
I longed for other humans
and kept on looking
without blinking.
There was the sun
and there were rocks.

There were a few trees,
but the only creature there was me.
It was a private room without walls.
All I did was just stand or lie on the ground.
Madly I imagined
that I had a woman there beside me,
making her bear children
and building a family.

Telescope

Since the scene was too far away
I looked through a telescope.
What I saw in the round peephole was
a grassy plain,
a horse, and a woman.
When I looked more carefully,
the woman was being ravished by the horse.
The horse was rearing on his hind legs,
holding the woman in front.
The naked woman, unable to break away,
was pressed under the horse's belly.
The horse raised his long neck proudly,
looking at me with his brown eyes.
I was sucked into his eyeballs
and dissolved into the round landscape
together with the horse and the woman.

Tomioka Taeko | (1935–)

TOMIOKA TAEKO was born in Osaka. In 1957, with money her father had given her as a student majoring in English at Osaka Women's University, she published her first book of poetry. The book, *Henrei* (*A Return Present*) won the eighth H-Shi Prize. A long poem, "Monogatari no Akuruhi" ("The Day after the Story"), published in 1960, won her the second Murou Saisei Prize. Her poetry is characterized by its whimsical narrative skill, influenced somewhat by the writings of Gertrude Stein, whose work she translated. Tomioka published her last book of poetry in 1970, turning thereafter to writing novels.

My Life Story

My mother and father
and the midwife
in fact, everyone who guessed
bet that I would be a boy,
so I determined to break from the placenta as a girl.

Then
everybody was disappointed,
so I became a boy for them.
Then everybody praised me,
so I became a girl.
Then
everybody bullied me,
so I became a boy.

When I reached adolescence,
my sweetheart was a boy,
so I reluctantly became a girl.
Then
everybody except my sweetheart became a girl,
so I became a boy
for everyone except my sweetheart.
I was sorry for my sweetheart,
but I'd become a boy.
Then he said he wouldn't sleep with me,
so I became a girl.

Meanwhile, several centuries passed.
This time
the poor started a bloody revolution
and were ruled solely by a piece of bread.
Then I became a medieval church
and walked about the alleys, giving out old clothes and rice balls,
saying, "Love, love will save us all."

Meanwhile, several centuries passed.
This time,
saying "The Kingdom of God has come,"
the rich and the poor became good friends.
Then
I scattered agitation bills from a private helicopter.

Meanwhile, several centuries passed.
This time
the bloody revolutionists were on their knees
in front of a rusty cross.
A light of order appeared amid the disorder.
Then
in a basement tavern
I played cards and had a drink
with Byron or Musset,
Villon or Baudelaire,
Hemingway or girls wearing black pants,
or seriously discussed such topics as libertines –
the kind peculiar to the country
in the East called Japan –
and we joked with each other, particularly
on such subjects as the synchronicity of love.

My father and mother
and the midwife
and everybody said I was a wonder child,
so I became a weak-minded child.
Since they said I was a fool,
I became an intellectual and built a house in the background,
and had too much physical energy to expend.

Since I got better known as an intellectual
in the background,
I began to walk up front.
The sidewalk
was the sidewalk of my father and mother.
Being perverse, I was perplexed
and troubled regarding the honor of a perverse person.
And so
I became a good girl for them.
I became a boy for my sweetheart,
refusing to allow his objections.

Just Between Us Two

You will make tea
and I will make toast.
In the meantime
we sometimes notice the bright red moon
early in the evening,
and sometimes we have a visitor,
who will never come back.
We close the shutter and lock it,
and make tea and make toast
and talk as usual
about the eventual possibility
of you burying me
or of me burying you in the yard,
and we will go out looking for food as usual.
The time will come
when you or I will bury
me or you
and the one left behind will sip the tea.
And only then for the first time will the one refuse to talk.
Your freedom has been
like a tale told by an idiot.

Amazawa Taijiro | (1936–)

AMAZAWA TAIJIRO was born in Tokyo. When he was three, his family moved to Manchuria, then returned to Japan in 1946. He graduated from Tokyo University, majoring in French literature. While there he started the magazine *Kyoku* (*Evil District*). One of the leading surrealist poets of the 1960s, he has said that poetry should neither serve its subject nor submit to it slavishly, and that the yardstick of poetry should be its "instability" and "uncertainty." Amazawa plays with the meanings of words, aiming at free expansion through a sustained succession of unusual images. Though difficult to understand, his style has earned him a reputation as one of the most important poets of Japan since the war.

City Poem

I like the city where clouds hang low, like clouds on a winter day,
and flow gently, almost touching the ground.
I like a city where stones and sand are dry
and only the tarred foot of a telephone pole is afloat.
I like a flag flapping in an unseen sky.
I like a city where I meet a dog that looks away at a crossroads.
I like a city where, as I walk, the doors are closed like mourning bands
and circle backward and backward without blinking.
I like a city where I often feel I might meet with a god
just around a street corner as I make the turn –
but as I go I find the clouds hanging a little higher –
a city where a single sound can be heard like two or three.
I like a city that watches me with eyes I cannot see.
I like a city where people remain death-still and pray in their homes,
while telephone poles, buildings, fenceposts, and trees are just
    like human beings.

A Song of Weeds

Impulsively, there in the meadow, I stood on one leg,
for there was no other way to become a weed.
the ears of a cloud protruded from the woods
and its suspicious eyes made me uncomfortable.
Gaily swinging my hands, which were bent like hooks,

I tried my best to wave like a weed.
Animals passed by without noticing me at all.
Standing there, shaking like that, I thought I was a weed.
I filled up my heart with my waving, thinking I was a weed
without any concept of my past or future.
In the steadily blowing wind, my eyes dried cool and black.
On my right, on my left, and in front of me,
all the way to the distant edge of the woods,
tall and tepid weeds were growing in droves.
They were really weeds.
I wanted to greet them.
I wanted to give them a signal by laughing,
but they paid absolutely no attention to me.
Worse, they didn't even look like me.
Each one was swaying on its separate stalk, looking at the sky
or squinting its eyes, helping the wind whistle, "*shree, shree.*"
It became obvious that I was not one of them.
Clouds were running through the blue sky.
The trees in the woods grew hushed and stood off in silent rows.
It was only me, standing there on one leg turning numb,
and not a weed, I thought.
I heard the song of weeds in me – I who was not a weed.

Late Summer for the Tree

Unable to bear the pain,
the tree tears off its own green leaves.
The pain is really an illusion caused by an eye left open.
But the hallucinated tree does not realize it.
As it tears off the leaves one by one,
the tree pulls its marrow-like self out of its trunk,
tasting the transparent bitterness of the sap in its wound.
Wind, don't rock it now.
Water, don't flow now.
The sweat oozing up to its bark soaks vainly into the moss,
and the blue of a thirsty flag simply gets tangled in the treetop.
Streets at the foot of the hill grow bewildered and turn steadily pale,
while from a hill of glass far beyond,
Argus, in a yellow building, turns his firm, cold eye at the tree.

Takahashi Mutsuo | (1937–)

TAKAHASHI MUTSUO was born in what is now Kitakyushu City, Fukuoka Prefecture and graduated from Fukuoka University of Education. His style and his materials are unusual and unorthodox. One of his frequent subjects is the world of the homosexual, and his work shows a broad interest in religious faiths. Two of his books to appear in English translation are *Poems of a Penisist* (Chicago Review Press, 1975) and *A Bunch of Keys* (The Crossing Press, 1984). Takahashi also writes novels and criticism.

The Dead Boy

I am a boy
who has suddenly fallen from the summit of a horrible boyhood
down into the darkness of the well, without ever knowing love.
The dark hands of the water strangle my delicate throat,
and countless gimlets of coldness bore in,
torturing my heart, which is wet as a fish.
Swelling like a flower with all those internal organs,
I move horizontally on the surface of underground water.
Out of the callow horn between my thighs
a helpless bud will soon sprout, crawling up
through the heavy earth with thin hands.
A tree like a pale face will sway some day
under painful light.
I want a lighted part in me
as much as the shadowed part.

I Need Nothing But...

I need nothing but a night filled with the rustling of pear trees.
I need nothing but the ribs of the sky still left burning,
    the heavy air, and a trumpet wet with saliva.
I need nothing but shiny skin, sweat,
    and downy hair all quivering together.
I need nothing but a tight jockstrap.
    a smelly phallus,

I need nothing but a night of enquiry against heresy
plus the smell of sperm and gore.

A Night for Valéry

(FROM "THE LUST OF THE EYES OR THE TRIBE OF EAGLES")

A stormy night will come sometimes.
In a room with its iron shutters pulled down tight,
a young man peers at the flames
burning in a form like rifles stacked against each other
on the iron frame in the fireplace;
or he reads a book on his lap,
and he hears the sound
of the bent branches of invisible trees touching
the outer side of the shutters.

Suddenly, very suddenly,
a brave determination rises
from among the crackling tree-like flames;
or an idea begins to gleam
from between the clean lines of the open book.
Music seethes violently in the young man's heart.
With all the sounds around him gone,
he is the center of a vacuum devoid of all meaning.

The following morning, he takes his coat from the peg by the door,
and quickly starts out on a trip without destination;
or he devotes himself to endless exploration in the forest of geometry.
His mother nervously pours tea for her son,
who has changed into a stranger overnight.

Watanabe Takenobu | (1938–)

WATANABE TAKENOBU was born in Yokohama. He completed the Ph.D. program in architecture at Tokyo University and is an architect by profession. He began to write poetry and submit poems to magazines in high school and became editor of the magazine *Kyoku* (*Evil District*) from 1964 to 1971. His poetry is modernistic and surreal, yet it has a firm sense of structure and is engaging to read. Watanabe's first book of poetry, *Mabushii Asa Sonota no Asa* (*A Glaring Morning and Other Mornings*), has been followed by other collections, and by critical essays on poetry, art, and jazz.

Vacation

Through a crevice
the fragments of numerous dreams could not fill up,
a white shoulder quickly passes –
a hot avalanche into the valley of my memory.

The wind blows furiously along your movement,
and in your loosened hair
the shadows of a hundred towns crumble.

Out of the sea of bedsheets spread everywhere
a small table floats up
as securely as a lifeboat,
and polished pieces of beautiful tableware
arrange themselves in place in the sunlight.

During our short, short vacation
pain slowly enters
always in the form of question.

A Sudden Noontime

In order to run
we want to assume a simple form
like a stag being chased
or a missile shining silver, but

our desires, being decorated
with kisses that spread out over the whole sky,
are more complex than any war.
When the morning's ominous smile, riding on the fast-rising tide
of consciousness, keeps expanding,
I cannot tell how fast we should run
to avoid wetting our feet.
When love or a lullaby carries us along
like a night train,
our shameless answer is always an instant faster
and a size bigger than the question.
The oversize bedsheets bulge
out of my sight.
Their fringe is unseen and unashamed.
Wrapped in them, the children are fast asleep
and their luminous ecstasy drops flakes of light as sharp as blades
rapidly receding forever.
When their sleep overheats
and finally forgets to wake,
it is you and I
who are left alone in the sudden noontime,
standing with our feet steeped in a sea of blood.

A Voice, or a Weekend

Violence makes the world transparent.
However,
on the other side of the broken mirror
there is no wilderness for heroes to stand on.
Down into the tender darkness
flaming sports cars plummet
one after another...headlong.

Sunday after Sunday
in the hot morning shower
my tiny heart suddenly cools down.
In the center of the white egg
that shines in its pale sea-green egg cup
a drop of coagulating blood falls,

like a stone,
outside the dream where you keep your sheep,
outside the dream where you kill your sheep,
outside the ring of the future that can be seen.

You better keep combing your hair slowly.
We may have to take the long way around yet.
It is not pain, but time
that tells of many a song, a fort, a committee,
and of the end of our pleasure.
It is not time but the smell of time.
It is not the smell, but perhaps
the silence,
a noisy silence
among the numerous wildly blossoming flowers,
various voices, one single voice,
a voice which we are gradually coming to,
your voice.

My voice.   My voice.

Yoshimasu Gozo | (1939–)

YOSHIMASU GOZO was born in Tokyo and graduated from Keio University with a major in Japanese literature. Inspired by the poetry of Ooka Makoto, he began writing poems at eighteen. His first book, *Shuppatsu* (*Departure*), was published in 1964. His second book, *Ogon Shihen* (*Golden Poems*, 1970), was a collection of strong imaginative poems that won the Takami Jun Prize. From November 1970 to April 1971, he studied in the Creative Writing Program at the University of Iowa. Uninhibited, passionate, and explosive, Yoshimasu's poetry ranks among the best in contemporary Japan – and in the world. A selection of his poems and prose pieces in English translation, *A Thousand Steps...and More*, has been published by Katydid Books, Oakland University, Michigan, 1987.

I Will Go Back

Joy recedes farther and farther every day.
You better count the joys you have seen in your lifetime.
These joys were, after all, flowers that bloomed
in the shade of misunderstandings and miscalculations.
As I sat on a dirty *tatami* mat,
silently touching the edge of a bowl,
and imagining the profile of a god I had never seen,
several years passed,
and my shadow, which is nothing but the accumulation of countless words,
seems to have taken its form.
People don't look at me the same way they look at a wild chrysanthemum.
I will no longer count on words.
I cannot hope to look out over a wide expanse of land
that I can really call a wilderness.
It is utterly useless
to ask man, a civilized creature, for fire.
If I can ever go back,
I will discover a log within my already exhausted soul
and carve it into an oar
which can travel across the stormy sea,
paddling through the stars hung in the sky.
And I will go back
to distant heavens

where lions and cyprinoid fish huddle together naked, whispering to each
    other.
I will go back.

The Plain

When the ancient sun rises on the eastern wall of my heart,
my whole body becomes a golden flute
and begins to play the melody
that controls nature.

I have been wandering like an elephant
in search of a place to die.
Like a canoe gliding through a springtime sea
I have been drifting
along the extended line of God's sigh.

The plain –
where the sun raises a shout like a rubber ball.
The plain – which is gentle and broad.
Ghosts smack their lips loudly on my upper arms.
Modern times whirl like sutras on my chest.

The plain.
This plain – where successive slaughters of flesh are covered
    by green ocean currents –
cannot be produced by my defeat or humiliation.
This plain where every substance begins to sputter and then
    breaks into flames by itself,
lurks in the territory of my victory.
Oh, my body,
be a golden flute and play a symphony.
Be a drop of gasoline
which can make every substance shed tears.
Open the doors,
naked nature.
I will go along with you to death,
to a glorious funeral,
to the celebration of death.

Today,
together with the sun that has risen on the eastern wall of my heart,
we will soar like wings
and let the music of fire drift over the vast plain.

Holding a Phantom Ship of Asia in my Right Hand

Holding a phantom ship of Asia in my right hand
and an ancient sun in my left,
I pray
again this morning.
In the middle of the altar
you gods pitch a tent and bloom profusely.
I ride on a large aged turtle,
cut down and throw away the body of my mother hanging on the setting sun,
and flow like an angry wave toward the Achilles' heel of nature.
Young lady, open up your radiant naked body.
My lump of flesh falls away
like flowers in the spring.
Rain like a woman's necklace falls on this brown-colored plain
where a three-legged wooden horse gallops by.
A television set barks sharply like a stray dog,
and my prayer
is like a windowpane inlaid with flesh
and is not so noble as a hymn or moonlight.
The waterdrops rage furiously.
On the back of poetical imagination
the sphere of winds moves like a secret ritual.
Guitars and friends bend
like the Parthenon.
The chaos is like an eddy.
Words are weirdly beautiful flowers
that can destroy all thinking, metaphysics, time, and history
at a single stroke.
May a child as cruel as the present age be brought forth
in the middle of my altar!
Until then
I will crawl over
to the bed of death

to awake
morning after morning.
Well,
this morning
this phantom ship trailing its shadow and the ancient sun
have withdrawn from my heart.
Now I will stand by the seashore and begin to howl,
send sand and poison arrows into the hearts of others,
and chase after some black panthers like a storm.

Yoshiyuki Rie | (1939–)

YOSHIYUKI RIE was born in Tokyo. She graduated from Waseda University with a major in Japanese literature, and joined the VEGA and Rekitei groups. Her poetry is surreal and succinct, with fantasy and reality standing curiously side-by-side. She has won prizes in both poetry and fiction, and she also writes children's stories. Her elder brother, Junnosuke, was a prominent novelist.

A Dream

In the gray garden
moonflowers
withered.

Wasn't it clear-eyed girls
singing in chorus
to the piano?

Moonlight was supposed to shine in
when I opened
the window.

I sit
with a funeral urn on my lap
in the hall.

A Dirge

Up the wide sky
the cabbage butterfly with injured wings will fly.

My little sister
is standing
under the spirea.
You will come
running.

An early summer rain
is swaying the spirea
with its fingertips.

Wearing a white dress,
I am looking up
at the sky
out of the window.
Please don't talk
in a pleasant voice
any more.

Moon in the Room

The moon is watching
the clown.

The clown
somersaults
and the moon smiles.

From its place high up
the moon is watching
the clown.

The cat is a moon in the room.
When the moon quietly disappears at dawn
it will take the clown along.

Tsuji Yukio | (1939–)

Tsuji Yukio was born in Tokyo and graduated from Meiji University in 1963, with a major in French literature. Tsuji is one of the few Japanese poets who can write unpretentious humorous verse. His poems often present his everyday experiences with amusing clarity, combining his wit and his personal warmth in a good-natured, casual tone.

You Come from the Other Side...

You come from the other side
and I come
from this side.
We say only, "Hello,"
and part, just like that.
Is this what we call a meeting?

When I go into the country, there are strawberries
in strawberry gardens,
vegetables in vegetable gardens.
I have a farmer friend,
and so I am a non-farmer friend
of my farmer friend.

"Well," we say to each other,
"we will always hang around like this.
We will go on just like this, won't we?"
After our twenties our thirties will come,
then later we'll be in our forties."

"Yeah. There's a riot in a distant country,
and yesterday a hundred people got killed, and today
another hundred will be killed. Or should I say
they will kill another hundred?"

I go back to my apartment and drink
all by myself.
Now I fold my arms,
now I tilt my head,

now I peer into the darkness
outside, where nothing is visible,
occasionally closing my eyes. Is this
the right attitude toward living?

Flowers

on the slope of the embankment
by the side
of the railroad track
at Ochanomizu Station

many little
yellow flowers bloom
in spring

in the morning
pressing our faces
against the train windows

we look at them

Dinner

These thin, yellow ivory chopsticks
I am using now
may perhaps be made from the bone of a horse,
but if they are really ivory, they once belonged
to a gigantic elephant that strutted
in a fleet-like herd far away in the African savannah.
When the elephant was shot between the eyes or through the ear,
he must have pointed his tusks at the tiny hunter,
his final, angry bellow echoing in the African sky,
setting giraffes, zebras, and rhinos running in stampede.
Even ants, sloths too, must have run wild.
It is always the vultures that remain at the scene
waiting for the picture-taking to come to an end,
circling very patiently,

observing,
waiting.
Ah, animals with whom I haven't talked
heart-to-heart,
you, friends,
I cannot tell at whom I should point my tusks,
nor whose death I am waiting for, but I am just eating,
hoping that a strong body nurtures a strong mind –
picking up the cow-meat with chopsticks made of an African elephant's tusk,
picking up a firefly squid
of the sea
whose eyes are somewhat protruded,
you elephant,
or perhaps
the bone of a horse.

Osada Hiroshi | (1939–)

Osada Hiroshi was born in Fukushima Prefecture and graduated from Waseda University in 1963, with a major in German literature. He first submitted poems in the early 1960s to magazines such as *Keshi* and *Chikyu*. His student days were marked by turmoil over the pros and cons of the U.S.–Japan Mutual Security Treaty. His first book of poetry, *Warera Shinsenna Tabibito* (*We, the Fresh Travelers*, 1965), reflected in vivid images the anxieties, loves, and struggles of young people in the hectic 1960s. Osada also writes critical essays about English, American, and modern Japanese literature, as well as children's literature, film scripts, and radio plays.

Looking for Spring

It is the time
when warm April rain
falls fast, relaxing the hard earth's muscles.
It is the time when seeds hidden deep
in the cold earth try to stand up
toward fulfillment,
trying to take shape,
and impatiently grope
for the hands of the sun.

It is the time
when intense sensitivity, bubbling up
in search of the center,
hugs the empty feeling
and sets the heart's edge suddenly upright.
The water grows warmer and richer,
making the sunlight stronger,
prompting the process.
Old roots revive new tension with the ground.

And the growing fibrils loosen words
that have been bound up in the hard earth,
restoring their gentleness.
At the end of the throat
into which births and deaths slip, tangled together,

the spirit of winter weakens,
and the force that is trying to lift the voice
comes calmly, steadily, through the green.

Then, will the force concentrate? the situation change?
What one wants to say is always the same.
But the words are not always the same.
We bring our mouths to the tips of the tender leaves
and drink the water dripping there.
Making sure of our love this way,
we explore the depth of sensitivity
in the time and shadow of noon,
which are filled with an increase of laughter.

About Love

I don't know the weight of a polished rifle
nor the sharp noise of strafing.
I don't know the bitter glare of silver wings
streaking the image of death across reaches of blue sky,
nor the coldness of the soldier of fog
who lay with his tired feet thrown into a burning sea.
The strange glare in the eyes
of those who talk about these things makes me
very uneasy.
     But today
our love turned the direction of their eyes.

     I found out later,
but it really was a mistake
thinking we could understand each other
when we met for the first time.
When dusk steals in, putting its front paws together,
after the day is done,
we walk slowly, carrying a handful of fatigue
and entwining our arms,
down the stone pavement along a dirty canal
over which the wet smell of old oil steadily crawls.
Then what we share with each other

unconsciously,
through slight warmth,
is the small territory of our hearts trying to be kind to each other.
(What more could we do?)

*

*   *

It's not a question of believing or not believing
or doing this or that.
Our duty is to live on, by whatever means,
to live, fighting against the malice of death.
"I will put a fragrant flower
in your hair,
so give me a gentle kiss on the forehead in return";
I sometimes say such things
without even blinking.
Is it a symbol of gentleness
or the emptiness of this sentimental age?

But being only ourselves,
we should represent the fate
which chose us, as long as we live, by doing whatever we do.
Nobody can choose a different time, a different action.
We keep silent or cry out
toward the nameless world
hung on the lips
and begin to step
little by little in the direction where our weight asserts itself,
and we finally become action itself,
no matter how ugly it may be.
We can do nothing but live our history and its deep meaning,
which are becoming sharply pointed, while burning white,
with our hearts quavering and warm – we....

Our love cultivates a process.
Better, the process itself brings us to the nature of love.
Keep it going, keep it going we must.
In the sheer act of keeping it going
we frolic with each other like kittens, snuggling up close.

Sea of Many Islands

Just as the blue of the sky that seems to smell so sweet
robs all the season's memories
of the sun's color,
we are lovers,
ever-fresh travelers!
Fresh stones and water
spread in the depths of fresh eyes. Fresh
urban civilization. Fresh islands, dripping,
are scattered like grapes.
Shellfish wake, dolphins glisten,
and those who are killed in old, old wars
slowly raise their heads,
and the fresh sea is in our kisses.

Ah, how strange it is
that the world is so fresh and so eternal.

EDWARD LUEDERS taught at the University of Utah for twenty-six years, serving as director of the Creative Writing Program and editor of *Western Humanities Review*. He is the author of eleven books, including *The Clam Lake Papers* (meditations and poetry on the interplay of nature and human thought), and presently works as a jazz pianist.

KORIYAMA NAOSHI was born in Kikai Island, Kagoshima Prefecture, in southern Japan in 1926 and studied English literature at Kagoshima Normal College, the University of New Mexico, and the State University of New York at Albany. He is professor of English at Toyo University in Tokyo and author of several volumes of poetry. He presently lives in Kanagawa.

BOOK DESIGN by John D. Berry. Composition by Typeworks. The typeface is Minion multiple master, designed by Robert Slimbach as part of the Adobe Originals type library. Minion is based on typefaces of the later Renaissance, but is derived from no single source. Slimbach designed Minion in 1990, then expanded it in 1992 to become a multiple master font – the first to include a size axis for optical scaling. Printed by Edwards Brothers.

Index of authors' names

Index of Titles